PINAKOTHEK
MUNICH

PINAKOTHEK
MUNICH

Newsweek / GREAT MUSEUMS OF THE WORLD

NEW YORK, N.Y.

**GREAT MUSEUMS
OF THE WORLD**

Editorial Director—Carlo Ludovico Ragghianti
Assistant—Giuliana Nannicini
Translation and Editing—Editors of ARTNEWS

PINAKOTHEK
MUNICH

Texts by:

Roberto Salvini
Raffaele Monti
Licia Ragghianti Collobi
Anna Pallucchini
Gian Lorenzo Mellini

Design:

Fiorenzo Giorgi

Published by

NEWSWEEK, INC.
& ARNOLDO MONDADORI EDITORE

Library of Congress Catalog Card No. 69-19062

© 1969—Arnoldo Mondadori Editore—CEAM—Milan

© 1969—Photographs Copyright by Kodansha Ltd.—Tokyo

INTRODUCTION

WOLF–DIETER DUBE
Curator, Alte Pinakothek

He who enters the Alte Pinakothek in Munich as a visitor, who wanders observantly through the halls and chambers, who does not allow himself to be captured by one work of art alone, but who rather tries to comprehend the compositition of the entire collection, that visitor will make some remarkable observations. He will perceive that many collections are without equal anywhere in the world; for example, the magnificent selection of early German painting, with works by Altdorfer, Dürer and Grünewald, or the splendid and unbelievably rich Rubens collection. On the other hand some epochs or schools are poorly represented or not to be found at all. This cannot be coincidence when one realizes that the paintings displayed in the Alte Pinakothek — Old Picture Gallery — are the best of the rich treasure of the Bavarian rulers. This treasure was brought together over a period of more than three hundred years by the sovereigns of the House of Wittelsbach and already comprised about eight thousand pictures at the time of the laying of the cornerstone of the Alte Pinakothek in the year 1826. The paintings in the Alte Pinakothek reflect not only the passion of the royal art collectors, they are at the same time a testimony of the artistic activity of the Bavarian ruling house.

The original collection was formed by an elaborately laid out cycle of antique and Christian historical subjects that Duke Wilhelm IV of Bavaria had commissioned in the years 1528 to 1540. Of this collection, the Netherlands' doctor and historian Samuel Quickelberg wrote in 1565:

"I should not like to miss the opportunity at this point to advise the best friends of art what a predilection for the honoring of excellent paintings Duke Wilhelm IV of Bavaria, the exceedingly understanding father of Duke Albrecht, has shown. For in his larger garden in Munich he has commissioned certain works by the best German artists and in fact the most wonderful products of their art are entered in a kind of honorable competition, in which he suggested the dimensions of each work. Strangers who come to Munich look at and admire these pictures with the highest degree of respect."

The most significant among these original paintings, which glorify manly virtue and bravery and represent the deeds of famous women, is Altdorfer's *The Battle of Alexander*. One must see, however, that the primary concern of the royal commissioner was the essential content, an exemplary illustration of history, as it revealed itself from a humanistic point of view. In this light also are to be understood the royal portraits, which the Duke commissioned by Barthel Beham, as well as the small gallery of portraits of court ladies, which his wife Jacobëa established. It was not supposed to be and could not be a gallery of paintings in the present meaning of the word. Also the remaining notable pictures owned by Wilhelm IV, such as Altdorfer's *Story of Susanna* and Dürer's *Lucretia,* were certainly selected under the aspect of the glorification of history.

Wilhelm's son, Duke Albrecht V (1550–1579) developed a pronounced collector's bent, even though his special predilection was for music. Albrecht's strong passion for collecting, to which most of the art collections of Munich owe their origin, set in motion a host of humanistic scholars, among them the famous Jakob Strada, who endeavored to bring together for their prince everything that could be found relating to art objects, curiosities and books. Even though some of the acquisitions of that period could not withstand critical observation — among the antiques, for instance, there were numerous forgeries — yet Albrecht did not in any way go about his task lightly. Whenever possible the Duke tried not only to purchase collections but at the same time to draw collectors and experts into his service. In this way the historian Samuel Quickelberg had come to Munich to draw up the theory and plan for the ducal *Kunstkammer,* or Chamber of Art, and he published this in 1565. In 1563 the building of the *Kunstkammer,* today's Mint, was begun. The objects brought to this place represented artistic value in part only. More important was its uniqueness, its specialty as a part of a theater of wisdom, of a gigantic *teatrum mundi,* theater of the world. The comprehensive knowledge of man and the world was served there equally by paintings, show-pieces, aborted fetuses, wonders of nature, manuscripts, maps, articles of clothing, etc., above all, however, by the curiosities, among which neither the half of a head of a satyr nor corn "rained from heaven" were missing. For the collection of antiques, however, no more room was to be found, and a separate building, the Antiquarium, was erected for it in the Residence between 1569 and 1571.

When Johannes Fickler, who had entered the Bavarian service after he had transferred his coin collection to the *Kunstkammer* began to take a first inventory of the Chamber of Art, he recorded 778 paintings. According to the nature of the collection, there were 579 portraits among them while only 58 pictures portrayed religious themes. Most numerous were series of portraits of Roman Emperors, of Greek and Roman poets and philosophers, of ancient heroes, of Dutch women and maids, of jesters and dwarfs, of murderers and criminals. Characteristic of the late 16th century also is the fact that in the inventory the names of the artists are given for only nine paintings; on the other hand, detailed descriptions are added to those exhibited, as in this entry.

"A portrait of a bloodthirsty murderer called Christoph Froschamer, from Wagingen of the Archbishopric of Salzburg, who with his own hand committed 345 murders and over 400 murders with his company, and who was executed at Wels in Austria in the year 1579."

With Maximilian I (1597–1651) — in the year 1623 the first Bavarian duke to attain electorship — a complete change took place. He was not only the highest ranking prince of his time, who took over the leadership of the Catholic party in the Thirty Years' War and whose political activity spanned all of Europe, he was at the same time a highly cultured, learned and even fanatic art collector, who was himself a dilettante at painting and one who found relaxation at the turning-lathe. Maximilian set a new standard of royal collecting activity. The interest of his predecessors, which was focused purely on the object, no longer touched him; only artistic considerations now determined the direction of his enthusiasm for collecting. In connection with the building of the Residence, Maximilian had installed from 1611 on in the vicinity of his bedchamber a *Kammergalerie,* or Chamber Gallery, a long, rectangular hall with a northern exposure. Here the most important pieces of the *Kunstkammer* and his own acquisitions were arranged.

An inventory of this gallery begun in 1628 names 117 paintings of which 68 are labeled with the names of artists. The inventory begins with the description of the works of Albrecht Dürer. Indeed at that time Dürer already belonged to those artists whose works should not be missing from any court gallery; yet only two princes left no stone unturned in their attempts to bring works of his hand into their possession. One was the Emperor Rudolf II; the other, Maximilian. For him, Dürer was the highest standard. When in 1614 he negotiated, in vain unfortunately, for a painting by Michelangelo, he offered as a reason the observation that "several of Michelangelo's works are praised above Dürer's." His persistent endeavors were actually successful in bringing together the most beautiful and most comprehensive collection of works of Albrecht Dürer. To the *Lucretia* which he had inherited, next came the *Lamentation over the Dead Christ* from the Nürnberg collection of Imhof. The political power of the Elector caused the city of Nürnberg shortly thereafter to deliver the *Paumgartner Altarpiece* to Munich, although not twenty years earlier a similar request of the Emperor Rudolf II had been "stiffly denied." Exactly the same fate befell the Dominicans in Frankfurt, who sold the *Heller Altarpiece* to Maximilian in 1614. Even though they had previously refused all the offers of the Emperor and of other princes, the friars could no longer deny the wish of the Bavarian Duke, the leader of the Catholic League. Unfortunately, this masterpiece of Dürer's was destroyed in the fire of 1729 in the Residence. And however hard they resisted and resorted to all imaginable tricks, the town fathers of Nürnberg finally had to sell to the Bavarian Elector the *Four Apostles*. Dürer eventually became an instrument of politics, whereby some persons even tried to offer his works to the Elector in order to get a political reward. Even the Emperor's generals were instructed to be on the lookout for pictures by Dürer for Maximilian. Eleven works of Dürer's are recorded in his inventory of the *Kammergalerie*.

Maximilian's interest in the remaining masters of the early German school was less pronounced. Italian painting was represented by only five pictures, among them, however, a Madonna by Raphael, which also burned in 1729. More extensive were the acquisitions of Netherlands paintings, among them those of contemporary artists. Finally, four large hunting scenes by Rubens were bought and with these the foundation of the great Rubens collection was laid. The first important collector of paintings among the Wittelsbach family had, therefore, already staked out the boundaries of the future collection. A sudden end was in store for Maximilian's collecting activity, however, when in 1632 the Swedes occupied Munich and plundered and destroyed all the art treasures that had not been hidden away.

The reign of the Elector Ferdinand Maria brought a breathing space to the land after the great war. A general activity of construction caused the interest in art collections to subside. When Maximilian II Emanuel came to the throne in 1679, Bavaria was drawn right into the midst of current European controversies. The new ruler, who also became Stadtholder of the Spanish Netherlands, was ambitious to become Holy Roman Emperor and saw his son made the heir to the Spanish crown. Max Emanuel used art as an acceptable representation of his political claims. The construction of the mighty *Galerieschloss,* Gallery Castle, in Schleissheim was begun and art treasures without measure were accumulated there. Max Emanuel, who was a passionate collector as well as a politician led astray by illusions, knew no bounds in this area. Even after the War of the Spanish Succession ended unhappily for him, when he had lost his land, and barely managed to eke out an existence in France, even when his servants left him because of hunger, he still kept several artists in attendance and planned great projects with them.

Max Emanuel was successful in a most important acquisition when he bought from Gisbert van Ceulen, the art agent of Antwerp, 101 paintings for 90,000 guilders, a sum that was not completely paid until 1774. No fewer than twelve paintings by Rubens, among them three portraits of Helena Fourment, thirteen pictures by Van Dyck, including the equestrian portrait of Charles I of England, eight by Brouwer, ten by Jan Bruegel, four by Claude, five by Wouwerman, still lifes by Snyders, Fyt, Boel among others and not least Murillo's *Gambling Beggar Boys* came to Munich in this way. It is true that in 1706 the Duke of Marlborough, the great victor of the War of the Spanish Succession, had the Emperor give him several of the pictures, among them the equestrian portrait of Charles I, which today belongs to the National Gallery in London.

Bavaria was returned to Max Emanuel in 1714 by the Peace of Rastatt. Although the debts had increased to thirty million guilders, the interrupted work on the construction of the castles was resumed at once. Unbroken was the will of the Elector, who not even then gave up his political dreams nor his passion for collecting. According to an account of Father Pierre de Bretagne from the year 1722, the best experts of that day asserted that there was "no greater, richer or more extensive gallery, none better stocked with all that is superior in all of Europe." And indeed, the collection in the *Galerieschloss* in Schleissheim must have conveyed an exceedingly rich and magnificent impression. In the Grand Gallery hung the show-pieces of the group acquired by Gisbert van Ceulen: Titian's *Charles V Seated;* seven works by Veronese; by Rubens, the *Portrait of Jan Brandt, Diana's Return, Mars Crowned by Victory,* and *Jesus and John the Baptist as Children;* portraits by Van Dyck; and additional works by Seghers, Snyders and Boeckhorst. How much the Elector preferred the Netherlands school of painting can also be seen in the fact that two of its most beautiful pictures hung in his bedroom: *Massacre of the Innocents* by Rubens and *The Rest on the Flight to Egypt* by Van Dyck. In the room of the Dutch and Flemish paintings, on the other hand, were no fewer than 163 pieces, among them twelve Brouwers, sixteen Teniers, twelve Frans van Mieris, nine Wouvermans, eight Dous and thirty-six Bruegels. And all of this was only a part of the collection. The Residence in Munich, Nymphenburg and other castles contained such treasures as the sixteen sketches of the Medici Series, *Meleanger and Atalanta* and *Love Carves the Arrow* by Rubens; portraits by Van Dyck; *Olympus* by Abraham Janssens; three Pouissins; *The Melon and Grape Eaters* by Murillo; Titian's *The Vanity of Earthly Things* and *The Crowning with Thorns;* Tintoretto's *Gonza Cycle* and Reni's *Apollo Flaying Marsyas,* to mention only a few. This was the amazing inheritance that Max Emanuel — in spite of all political reverses — left at the time of his death in 1726.

Since his son, Karl Albrecht (1726–1745), continued to follow the disastrous politics of his father, an increase in the collection was out of the question. He did succeed, however, in being crowned Holy Roman Emperor as Karl VII, but he was subsequently banished from his land and found a poor sanctuary in Frankfurt. His successor, Maximilian III Joseph, assumed a mountain of debts of forty million guilders and could, therefore, think only of putting that which was available in order and making it, as far as possible, serviceable for educational and cultural purposes. In 1775 the first printed catalog of the gallery in Schleissheim appeared; it describes 1,050 paintings. Besides these, more than 300 paintings were to be found in Nymphenburg, approximately 550 in Dachau, close to 700 in the Residence in Munich, 194 in Lichtenberg and 176 in Laufzorn.

The step towards making it an open, accessible gallery was made by the Elector Karl Theodor, who, in 1777, after the Bavarian line had died out, took possession of the total inheritance of the Bavarian and Palatinate lands. Between 1780 and 1781 he had a gallery building erected in Munich, the so-called *Hofgartengalerie,* Gallery of the Palace Garden, in which 700 paintings from various castles were combined. "It is heart-stirring to see a crowd of pupils working there; how everyone rejoices that the gallery now stands open for all people," wrote a contemporary.

Karl Theodor also valued baroque Netherlands art above all else, so his acquisitions did not change the character of the collection. More important for the Munich Gallery, however, was the fact that Karl Theodor, who had previously resided in Mannheim, brought along the Gallery of Mannheim and that of Düsseldorf as an inheritance. There were 758 pictures from Mannheim, again preponderantly those of the Netherlands school, most of them small in size. Among them were the *Sacrifice of Isaac* and *Holy Family* by Rembrandt; portraits by Ravesteyn and Maes; genre scenes by Ostade, Steen, Ter Borch, Dou, Mieris, Netscher and many others; and also the *Shepherd's Scene* and the *Portrait of a Young Man with Beret* by Rubens; two pictures by Van Dyck; four by Brouwer and numerous works by Jan Bruegel.

The Düsseldorf Gallery had substantially fewer works, with only 348 pictures; yet it was rightly esteemed, because of its wealth of excellent works by Rembrandt, Rubens and Van Dyck, as one of the most beautiful and important collections of Europe. The Elector Johann Wilhelm of the Palatinate (1690–1716) had created it. Since his means were limited — large parts of the Palatinate with Heidelberg had been destroyed by the French — he concentrated his attentions on a few pictures and above all he used his family connections quite skillfully. His wife, Anna Maria Ludovica, the daughter of Cosimo III of Tuscany, brought to Düsseldorf as a dowry Raphael's the *Canigiani Holy Family* and the *Holy Family* by Andrea del Sarto, and as gifts came works by Baroccio, Domenichino and Lanfranco from Florence. Of course, as a return gift Johann Wilhelm gave self-portraits by Rubens and Van Dyck to the Uffizi Gallery. He had his brother-in-law, the King of Spain, give him the *Reconciliation of Jacob and Esau* by Rubens. Johann Wilhelm spared no effort in acquiring paintings by this master. In order to preserve the altars that his grandfather Wolfgang Wilhelm of Pfalz-Neuburg had ordered from Rubens for the Jesuit church in Neuburg, even the Pope was troubled again and again, finally with success. Ultimately Johann Wilhelm had forty-six works by Rubens in his possession, among them the large and the small *Last Judgment,* the *Fall of the Rebel Angels, Christ and the Repentant Sinners,* the *Crucifixion,* the *Madonna in a Wreath of Flowers,* the *Martyrdom of St. Sebastian,* the *Battle of the Amazons,* the *Rape of the Daughters of Leucippus,* the *Drunken Silenus* and above all the *Honeysuckle Arbor*. He had brought together twenty-five pictures by Van Dyck, and Rembrandt's Passion series and his *Adoration of the Shepherds* likewise belonged to the treasures of the collection.

This was not enough, however. When the Elector Karl Theodor died in 1799, the line of Pfalz-Zweibrücken came to rule with Maximilian IV Joseph, who was crowned King of Bavaria in

1806 as Maximilian I. The Zweibrücken collection included some one thousand paintings, predominantly by Dutch masters, which now were also transmitted to Munich. In addition, most of the French pictures of the Alte Pinakothek stem from this collection, since the relations between Zweibrücken and Paris had been very close. Max IV Joseph had been a general in the service of the French until his accession to the Bavarian throne.

However, there were not only gains, but losses as well, even though the collections were almost constantly in flight or in hiding during the wars of the revolution. A total of seventy-two paintings were carried off to Paris by the French in 1800, of which only twenty-seven could be won back again. Among others lost to French museums were: by Rubens, the *Adoration of the Magi* in Lyon; the *Boar Hunt* in Marseilles; *Tiger and Leopard Hunt* in Bordeaux (which later burned); the *Boar Hunt* by Paul de Vos in the Louvre and Tintoretto's *Madonna with Saints* in Lille.

Secularization brought a renewed expansion of the collection by means of the seizing of the church lands in Bavaria and in the Bavarian Tyrol. Close to 1,500 pictures came into the possession of the Munich collection in this way. The early German section was enriched above all by the *Kaisheimer Altarpiece* of Hans Holbein the Elder, two Passion scenes by Wolf Huber, Dürer's *Mary as Mother of Sorrows*, the wings of the *Laurentius Altarpiece* and the *Kirchenväter Altarpiece* by Michael Pacher, altars by Marx Reichlich, the *Disputation of St. Erasmus and St. Maurice* and the *Mocking of Christ* by Grünewald, Cranach's *Crucifixion*, Altdorfer's *Mary in Glory*, by Baldung the *Portrait of the Palatinate Count Philipp* and the *Nativity* and by Pleydenwurff a *Crucifixion*. In addition to these came the *Woman of the Apocalypse* by Rubens from the cathedral of Freising, *Christ at the House of Martha and Mary* by Tintoretto as well as his gigantic *Crucifixion*, the *Adoration of the Magi* by Tiepolo, the *Peasant Woman* by Pieter Bruegel the Elder and the *Self-Portrait* by Carel Fabritius.

The growth of the collection by coincidence and according to the taste of the reigning sovereign was brought to an end by King Ludwig I (1825–1848), while he was still crown prince. He was no longer driven merely by the enthusiasm of an art patron, but allowed himself to be guided by historical and political considerations. Thanks to him alone, works of Giotto, Fra Angelico, Albertinelli, Botticelli, Raffaellino del Garbo, Fra Filippo Lippi and Filippino Lippi, of Ghirlandaio and Perugino and above all Raphael's *Madonna della Tenda* and *Tempi Madonna* adorn the Alte Pinakothek. In making his acquisitions, Ludwig always had in mind the plan of a grand new building for the collection, whatever did not appear absolutely necessary for this was refused; whatever was worthy of pursuit was sought with never slackening perseverance, even if decades passed. In 1815 he had already recognized the eminent importance of the Boisserée collection, which consisted primarily of masterpieces of the early Netherlandish and Cologne schools. The focus of the extensive collection, which included 216 paintings, was the *Altar of the Three Kings* by van der Weyden. Not until he was king in 1827 did Ludwig succeed in acquiring it, though the kings of Prussia and Württemberg had both failed in their attempts to get the work. It was only consistent with his earlier purchases that one year later King Ludwig I also bought the 219 paintings of the South German and Swabian schools belonging to the Wallerstein collection. Thus he created in Munich the most important and most complete gallery of early German painting.

The long planned new building for the collection, which Ludwig called the *Pinakothek,* Picture Gallery, was begun in the year 1826 and was opened to the public in 1836. With this, not only was the building finished, but the collection in it was essentially completed as far as the king was concerned. None of his successors even attempted a continuation or expansion of it. Ludwig then turned to the art of his day, to the founding and enlarging of the Neue Pinakothek, or New Picture Gallery.

At a time when important galleries were being established in other places, the Alte Pinakothek sank into stagnation. Academic painters were charged with its management, and about their activity an official of the Ministry of Education reports in his memoirs:

"I cannot hide the fact that it always seemed strange to me, whenever I visited the Gallery, to find the directors and curators of our galleries as a rule only in their offices, furnished as workshops, at the easel where they, as in times past, painted pictures to be sold, and considered the administration of the Gallery merely as a matter of secondary importance."

Thus it was possible that in 1852, 971 paintings from this repository were auctioned off for only 8,672 guilders, among them a Dürer portrait that was virtually thrown away for 30 guilders because money was needed to complete a portrait gallery with copies.

Only in 1875 was an art expert for the first time called to be director of the gallery. Finally, in 1888, a limited purchasing budget was put at his disposal. However important the single acquisitions have been since that time — Leonardo's *Madonna,* works by Signorelli and Antonello da Messina, the *Portrait of Willem Croes* by Frans Hals, El Greco's *Disrobing of Christ,* Guardi's *Concert,* Pieter Bruegel's *Fool's Paradise, Utopia,* and *Land of the Idle,* Tintoretto's *Venus, Vulcan and Mars* and Rembrandt's *Self-Portrait as a Young Man,* to mention only a few — new centers of attraction could hardly be organized. The Alte Pinakothek remained and shall continue to remain a testimony to the appreciation and cultivation of art by the Bavarian princes.

GERMANY

ST. VERONICA MASTER. *St. Veronica with the Holy Kerchief.*
This painting is one of the old German masterpieces that most influenced the revival of interest in the art of the primitives during the Romantic period. While still in the collection of the Boisserée brothers at Heidelberg, it aroused the admiration of Goethe (1815), who noted in the arrangement of the groups of angels "enough artistic skill to satisfy the highest standards of composition." He also appreciated the painter's "ability to abstract, placing his figures in accordance with three-dimensional representation, yet succeeding in imbuing the whole work with symbolic thought."

More than a German masterpiece, it is one of the great works of early 15th-century European painting and is connected with the broad current of the International Gothic style. This painting, in fact, sums up the richness and refinement achieved by the European Gothic in its long development, leading from Siena to Avignon, and from Avignon to Paris and Burgundy. But a special connection is apparent between the panel from Cologne and the painting of Dijon, where — it is opportune to recall — a painter called Hermann von Köln (Cologne) worked for Philip the Bold in the Chartreuse de Champmol around 1402. All of this tradition is interpreted by the St. Veronica Master with subdued melodic subtlety. All over the composition, under the rich, enamel-like color, there is a continual correspondence of rhythms, from the undulation of the kerchief to the radiating tiles and the pure lineal motives created by the two groups of angels. The St. Veronica Master is outstanding for his chaste and quiet lyricism, which gives him a very high place in the "courtly" art that around 1400 carried the richest ornamental aspects of the Gothic to its furthest limits.

MASTER OF THE TEGERNSEE PASSION. *Crucifixion. pp. 20–21*
The anonymous master is also the author of the altarpiece for the high altar in the Tegernsee monastery, which was executed in 1445–46 and is now divided among various museums (*Christ Carrying the Cross* is in the Alte Pinakothek). He is often identified — mistakenly it appears — with the painter Gabriel Mälesskircher. The present *Crucifixion* belonged to another complex, and seems to have been done somewhat earlier. A work that perhaps should be seen in relation to the painting of the Salzburg region, it has an archaic aspect not in the same sense as the International Gothic, but rather in a 14th-century tradition ultimately deriving from Giotto. Through the solid plasticity of the figures and the broad rotary movement, the painting achieves a nobly dramatic effect.

ST. VERONICA MASTER
Active in Cologne from 1400 to 1420
St. Veronica with the Holy Kerchief
(circa 1400) Pine panel; 37 3/4″ × 19″.
From St. Severin, Cologne, where it probably was the door of a reliquary shrine.

Pages 20–21:
MASTER OF THE
TEGERNSEE PASSION
Active in Munich between 1430 and 1450
Crucifixion (circa 1440–45)
Pine panel; 6′1 1/4″ × 9′7 3/4″.
Painted in grisaille

MASTER OF THE POLLING PANELS. *Two Panels from the Altarpiece of the Holy Cross.*

The anonymous master is probably to be identified with the painter Gabriel Angler, known by documents to have been in Munich from 1434 until about 1482 and to have died before 1486. The scenes represented read horizontally from left to right, starting at the top and going from panel to panel. In this sequence they show the following events: Duke Tessilo, accompanied by three equerries, goes hunting; a doe, ignoring the attacking dogs and the approaching hunter, paws at the ground where the tip of a cross appears; Tessilo sets out with a bishop for the place where the cross has been found; the cross is unearthed and blessed by the bishop, as Tessilo decides to establish the monastery of Polling at that spot. Like the panels of the *Altarpiece of the Madonna,* by the same painter and from the same Abbey of Polling, this work is very important historically, as it typifies the approach of southern German artists in the first half of the 15th century. Even more than in the *Wurzach Altarpiece* by Hans Multscher (or by the Swabian painter working with him), a rugged naturalism — in the coarse plasticity of the figures — is introduced into a spatial and compositional context that is still typical of the International Gothic style.

STEPHAN LOCHNER. *Nativity.* *p. 24*

Lochner was probably a native of Meersburg on Lake Constance, where it is known that his parents resided. After a journey to the Low Countries — deduced from the considerable traces of Flemish influence in his early works — Lochner established himself at Cologne about 1442, while still a youth. In the great Rhineland city he married and in 1447 was elected to the town council. He died in December, 1451, a victim of the plague.

We owe the recovery of his name to the businesslike care with which Albrecht Dürer recorded the details of his daily life. In his travel diary Dürer noted the five *weiss* that he gave as a tip to the custodian who opened the wings of the *Triptych of the Three Magi* for him in the chapel of the Cologne Rathaus. Fortunately he added the notation that the work was by "*maister Stefan zu Cöln.*" In 1852, Dürer's "Stefan" was identified by an archives researcher as Stephan Lochner, mentioned as a painter in a number of the town's documents. Lochner was also among the first German painters to be revalued by the Romantics. In 1805 Friedrich von Schlegel was already comparing the Virgin in the Rathaus triptych to Raphael's *Sistine Madonna* because of "the supernal, ideal beauty of the face." The enthusiasm of the literati soon reached such heights that an annoyed Goethe said of these ravings that "it is only to be hoped that the real merits [of the painting] will be given a historical and critical appraisal."

Goethe's hoped-for appraisal by now has been attained, with the recognition of this master's singular position between the International Gothic and Flemish naturalism, and his not always easy effort to strike a balance be-

MASTER OF THE POLLING PANELS
Active in Munich between 1434 and 1450
Two Panels from the Altarpiece of the Holy Cross
Pine panel; each 7'2 1/2" × 2'10 3/4".

tween these two cultural elements. Lochner's most coherent results are thus to be found mainly in his minor, or at least smaller, works, like this one in which all inconsistency between the two traditions is overridden by the purity of the new lyric quality. Rich linear and compositional rhythms and a discreet approach to a more "natural" vision of space and landscape blend felicitously in Lochner's quiet poetry.

STEPHAN LOCHNER. *SS. Catherine, Hubert and Quirinus.*
This painting is part of a youthful work that was probably executed soon after the painter established himself at Cologne, following his return from a journey to or a sojourn in Flanders. A familiarity with Flemish art is indicated by the obvious recollections of Jan van Eyck that are seen in the central panel (in Cologne), especially in the nudes that recall the Ghent polyptych. Here too there is clearly a search for an accord between the undulating Gothic linearity and the plastic and chromatic substance of the form, in the Flemish manner. In the harshness of the St. Quirinus there is some reference to Upper Rhenish painting and to Konrad Witz.

Left:
STEPHAN LOCHNER
Meersburg (Lake Constance)
circa 1410 — Cologne 1451
Nativity (circa 1440–45)
Panel; 14″ × 8 1/2″.
Recently acquired from a private collection in Bad Godesberg, formerly in Berlin.

Above:
STEPHAN LOCHNER
SS. Catherine, Hubert and Quirinus (wing of an altarpiece of the *Last Judgment* formerly in St. Lawrence, Cologne) (circa 1430)
Walnut panel; 47 1/4″ × 31 1/2″.
The central part is in the Wallraf-Richartz Museum of Cologne; the inner panels of the wings are in the Städel Museum, Frankfurt.

MARTIN SCHONGAUER. *Nativity*.

The dating of this work is uncertain because of the scarcity of material for comparison. The body of Schongauer's known work includes only one dated painting, the large *Madonna of the Rose Garden* of 1473, in the Collegiate Church, Cologne; a small number of little panels without dates; and the faded frescoes of the church at Breisach, on which the master was working in 1491, the year of his death. The small picture presented here would seem to be close to the little *Madonna* in Vienna, which because of its frank adoption of the Flemish manner of Rogier van der Weyden would in turn appear to be earlier than the Colmar panel.

The master's sparsely documented activity as a painter, however, cannot be considered apart from his much better known work as an engraver. His

training to a large extent took place in the print-making field. The lively and spirited engravings by the anonymous master known by the monogram E.S. served as Schongauer's point of departure. In his prints the new principle of linear dynamism elaborated by the Master of the Monogram E.S. is elevated from mere pleasing and spirited illustration to a high level of artistic achievement. Thus there is born, in line with the realistic approach of German painting in the second quarter of the fifteenth century, a new and more complex relationship with reality. It represents, moreover, a less contemplative and more actively endured human experience, with similarities in style and mental attitude to contemporary Florentine painting. In this little *Nativity,* Flemish influence, and in particular that of Rogier van der Weyden, is apparent in the highly subtle vibrancy of the lines, and in the chiseled forms under the lucid color. The vitality and freshness of the figures, the flowers and the landscape express an intimate and anxious lyricism. It is well known that in 1490 the young Dürer, on a long journey from his native Nürnberg, arrived at Colmar, where he hoped to get to know Schongauer, but arrived after the artist's death. And Michelangelo, as a boy, amused himself by coloring, or copying, a famous print by the "good Martin."

MICHAEL PACHER. *Four Fathers of the Church* and *St. Wolfgang Praying for a Miracle.*

Michael Pacher, wood sculptor and painter, citizen of Bruneck in the Carnic Alps, died at Salzburg while working on the great altarpiece for the Francis-

MICHAEL PACHER
Neustift (Novacella, near Bressanone)?
circa 1440 — Salzburg 1498
Four Fathers of the Church
Mediterranean pine wood; wings: 7'1"
× 2'11 3/4" each; central part: 7'1"
× 6'5 1/4". Interior of triptych with wings
opened. Dated by documents: 1482–83.
The four Fathers of the Church (from left
to right: St. Jerome, St. Augustine, St.
Gregory taking the Emperor Constantine
out of Hell, St. Ambrose) comprise the
interior of the open triptych. The scene
from the life of St. Wolfgang at right is
painted with three others (*Disputation of
St. Wolfgang, St. Wolfgang Surprises a
Thief* and *St. Wolfgang Obliges the Devil
to Hold his Missal*) on the outer panels of
the wings. The whole composition made up
the great altarpiece of the Altar of the
Fathers of the Church in the church of the
Neustift (now Novacella) near Bressanone,
and was executed between 1482 and 1483.

Right:
MICHAEL PACHER
St. Wolfgang Praying for a Miracle
Mediterranean pine wood; 7'1" × 2'11"
(the complete panel);
42 1/2" × 35 3/4" (the part reproduced
here).
Detail of outside panel of right wing.
Dated by documents 1482–83.

cans. He was familiar with the art of the Tyrol and Swabia, as well as with
that of northern Italy, especially the work of Mantegna and of Fra Filippo
Lippi. A great artist, Pacher anticipates Dürer to some extent in creating a
happy synthesis of 15th-century German and Italian art. His construction of
space, with its low viewpoint, is derived directly from Mantegna's work in
Padua and perhaps also from that in Mantua. But already in the altarpiece
from St. Wolfgang am Abersee (near Salzburg), which was commissioned
in 1471 and completed in 1481, Pacher's space shows a dynamism — even
in the quietest scenes — in which the linear fury of German art in the second half of the 15th century is resolved. Everywhere, Italian spatial perspective is expressed in a web of forceful lines.

In the present polyptych there are notably dynamic spatial effects. Note, for
instance, in *St. Wolfgang Praying for a Miracle* how the clear perspective
space, with its vanishing point just below the pointed arch of the door in the
background, is like a gravitational field. This is so because the composition
is built up on diagonals, in which the impetus of the flying angel is opposed
by the heavy volume of the saint in prayer. All this creates a sense of deep
and exalted drama, in the midst of the composition's eloquent silence. In the
powerful *Fathers of the Church,* where the tension of the intersecting forces
is circumscribed and compressed within a space — scooped out seemingly
by dint of the foreshortening of the objects in the foreground — the impression of unresolvable torment is much more intense. The planes of resplen-

dent metallic color bend and tense like sheets of metal under the hammer of the metalsmith. Lines and planes are composed in a system aiming to enclose their own dynamics in an unattainable balanced stability, creating effects that anticipate Dürer.

Aside from his more instinctive temperament, his more immediate relationship with the artisan tradition and his less intellectual concern, Michael Pacher, in his mental approach, is in fact close to Albrecht Dürer. Although there is no direct stylistic evidence, it would be interesting to imagine that the great painter from Nürnberg had stopped at Neustift (now Novacella) on his way south to Italy and had closely studied this great work of his worthy predecessor.

MARX REICHLICH. *The Visitation.*

This work is one of a series of four panels (the others represent the *Birth of the Virgin, Betrothal of the Virgin* and *Presentation in the Temple*) that originally formed the wings of a carved-wood altarpiece at Neustift. The date, inscribed on the panel showing the *Presentation in the Temple,* has sometimes been read erroneously as 1502, whereas it is actually 1511. A student of Michael Pacher, Reichlich combined his master's lessons with his own strongly poetic outlook. Compared to Pacher's compositions, the forms here are fuller and are softened by the intense color, full of modulations and reflections, that is very probably influenced by a direct knowledge of Venetian painting on the part of the artist. The landscape itself, with the overhanging mountain beyond the perspective of the portico, acquires a picturesque accent going beyond its spatial value. An intimate warmth, an atmosphere of confidential and moving conversation permeates the scene, which is affectionately situated between the Renaissance portico and the Gothic porch of a little Tyrolean town in the lee of the mountain.

MASTER OF THE ST. BARTHOLOMEW ALTARPIECE. *St. Agnes.*

This work also is one of a series of panels, belonging originally to an incomplete triptych dedicated to St. Bartholomew, whose figure is seen in the middle of the central panel. The wings of the triptych, which also are in the Alte Pinakothek, show St. John the Evangelist, St. Margaret, St. Christina and St. James the Less. Two other panels of the same size, in Mainz and London, have been tentatively identified as the exterior panels of the wings in Munich. It is this altarpiece, which comes from the church of St. Columba in Cologne, that has given the master his name.

Although he fits well into the refined atmosphere of the school of Cologne during the last decades of the 15th century, this painter, whose activity runs roughly from 1470 to 1510, was of Dutch origin. He was trained at Utrecht and shows affinities to — though he is not as great as — the Dutch artist known as the Master of the Virgo inter Virgines. His color is rich and elaborate, as is seen here in the refinement of the elegant harmonies between St. Agnes' deep blue mantle lined with pink and her brocaded tunic, and the studied relationship of those colors to the variously corresponding and con-

28

trasting hues of the two accompanying figures (not shown here). The painter is just as elaborately refined in his forms, which have a metallic, chiseled quality that suggests a mysterious correspondence with the painting of his Venetian contemporary, Crivelli. With this exquisite, "decadent" style the school of Cologne comes to an end.

MASTER OF THE LIFE OF THE VIRGIN. *The Birth of the*
Virgin. *p. 30*

In the second half of the 15th century, the school of Cologne, like many other German schools, was influenced by the second phase of Flemish painting. It was no longer the Master of Flémalle and Jan van Eyck, but Rogier van der Weyden and Dieric Bouts who served as examples. Still the pull of the old tradition and the fascination of Lochner's resplendent art continued to have their effect on the copious, sometimes even monotonous, production of the school. Among the entirely anonymous, arbitrarily named artists of this group, the author of these panels, who is also known to have executed

some of the numerous portraits from this period, is unquestionably outstanding. Concern with illustration — in the rendering of the rooms, in the description of the costumes and in the affable attitudes of the figures — is greater here than any properly stylistic commitment. Yet there is an undeniable poetic vein in the exact and affectionate description of this childbed scene and in the unexpected charm that emanates from the improbable perspective and the golden clarity of the colors.

MASTER OF THE LIFE OF THE VIRGIN
Active in Cologne from 1460 to 1480
The Birth of the Virgin (circa 1460)
Oak panel; 33 1/2″ × 41 1/4″.
One of seven panels — an eighth is in the National Gallery, London — from an altarpiece in St. Ursala, Cologne.

MASTER OF THE AIX–LA–CHAPELLE ALTARPIECE.

Madonna and Child.

This anonymous painter, who takes his name from a polyptych in the Cathedral of Aix-la-Chapelle, or Aachen, belongs to the last phase of the school of Cologne and derives from the Master of St. Severin and the Master of the Holy Family. Uneven and eclectic, he is a minor master who absorbed the Flemish influence current in the second half of the 15th century in Cologne. Yet, in some of his works, such as the *Adoration of the Magi* in Ber-

lin, he shows a harshness of stroke and a hardness of form that recall Martin Schongauer's graphic work and Dutch painting at the end of the century. It has an expressionistic, at times even a folk, character that is very different from the always more aristocratic Flemish painting. The artist's loud, clear and many-hued color is one of the most striking features of his painting. This *Madonna and Child* belongs among the best works created by the master, an achievement perhaps aided by the small size of the panel. It has a fine balance of compositional rhythms as well as a chromatic harmony between the ringing hues of the drapery and the luminosity of the landscape.

BERNHARD STRIGEL. *Portrait of Conrad Rehlinger's Children. p. 32*
This monumental group portrait (the age of each child is shown above his head) is a companion piece to the Alte Pinakothek's full-length portrait, of the same size, of the father of the family. Bernhard Strigel of Memmingen, descendant of a family of painters and wood sculptors, belongs to the Swabian school and was the pupil of the mild and dignified Bartholomäus Zeit-

32

BERNHARD STRIGEL
Memmingen 1460 — Memmingen 1528
Conrad Rehlinger's Children
Pine panel; 7'10 1/4" ×3'2 1/2".
Signed and dated 1517.

blom. Although fundamentally a traditionalist, Strigel felt the new currents of the times, and under the spell of the Renaissance movement in Augsburg gave his painting a solid and monumental, fully 16th-century expression.

HANS HOLBEIN THE ELDER. *Martyrdom of St. Sebastian.*
The central panel of a triptych from the chapel of St. Sebastian in Augsburg's church of the Holy Saviour, this work was actually commissioned by Magdalen Imhof for the Church of St. Catherine, where the altar on which

HANS HOLBEIN THE ELDER
Augsburg circa 1465 — Isenheim 1524
Martyrdom of St. Sebastian (1515–17)
Lime panel; 60 1/4″ × 42″.

33

it stood was consecrated in 1517. The original frame has disappeared, but it bore the artist's signature and the date 1516. Hans Holbein the Elder absorbed as much as he could of the robust tradition of Swabian painting and of the new ferment created by influences from Italy in Augsburg, the headquarters of the Fugger bank and a world financial center. Fundamentally, however, he remained a traditional painter, for painstaking craftsmanship always outshone the humanistic intelligence in his work. Although the composition of this painting is highly conventional and lacking in spatial clarity, it can be admired for its strength of line and fullness of form, as shown in the individualized definition of the figures. To a certain extent these techniques are a distant preparation for Holbein the Younger's great portraits.

HANS BURGKMAIR.   *St. John at Patmos.*
This is the central part of a triptych with swinging panels (the two St. Johns on the outer faces, St. Erasmus and St. Nicholas on the inner) dedicated to St. John the Evangelist. Hans Burgkmair was the pupil of his father, Thomas, a traditional Augsburg painter, and of Schongauer at Colmar. Like Dürer, he visited Italy, journeying to Venice for the first time before 1500 (as is deduced from his stylistic development). Very different in personality from his fellow artist from Nürnberg, however, he was stimulated by a superficial curiosity about the new and a snobbish desire to be up-to-date. A new maturity showing influence from Bellini, which is discernible in the Nürnberg *St. Sebastian Altarpiece* of 1505, suggests that by that year the artist had made another journey to Italy. A third visit to Venice may have taken place a little earlier than 1518, when Titian was painting his *Assumption* in the church of the Frari, for in the present *St. John Altarpiece* and the immediately following *Crucifixion Altarpiece* (also in the Alte Pinakothek) a new monumentality and a new intensity of color are apparent. The excited posture of the saint, the imposing landscape and the fantastic light lend a new, almost romantic, sentiment to these human and natural images. At the same time, through incisive line, they maintain a live sense of the precision and nervous vitality of German tradition.

ALBRECHT DÜRER.   *Portrait of Oswald Krell, Merchant of Lindau.*
p. 36
Along with his *Self-Portrait* in Madrid, this is undoubtedly the finest of the numerous portraits executed by Dürer between 1497 and 1500, following his return from his first sojourn in Venice. The figure stands out from the background with the greatest plastic effect and is turned slightly to the right, while the lively eyes look to the left. The form is built up, as if in layers of different materials, by the successive planes of color, the dense and luminous hues recalling Antonello, Gentile Bellini and the Murano artists. These colors range from the red of the curtain and the bronzed flesh color to the dark-hued costume, which is barely interrupted by the white tunic, and the light, luminous brown of the fur. Along with the coloring should be noted the highly linear rendering of the features of the face and the firm contours of the figure. The powerful physical presence conveyed by the robust plastic and chromatic construction thus coincides with the sharp spiritual energy

34

HANS BURGKMAIR
Augsburg 1473 — Augsburg 1531
St. John at Patmos
Pine panel; 60 1/4″ × 49 1/4″.
Signed and dated 1518.

ALBRECHT DÜRER
Nürnberg 1471 — Nürnberg 1528
Oswald Krell, Merchant of Lindau
(dated 1499)
Lime panel; 19 3/4" × 15 1/4".

expressed by the linear fabric. The glimpse of landscape to the left is also highly linear and is stratified in a succession of colors that correspond to those of the figure. Instead of representing a contemplative and escapist motive, as in the Flemish and Venetian traditions, this portrait supports and emphasizes the strong-willed tension, the almost aggressive spirit of the subject.

ALBRECHT DÜRER.   *Nativity.*   *p. 37*
                       St. George and *St. Eustace.*   *p. 38*
These are the central panel and wings of the *Paumgartner Altarpiece* which was erected, probably in 1503, at the end of the south aisle of the church of St. Catherine in Nürnberg. It was commissioned in honor and memory of Martin Paumgartner (died 1478) by his sons Stephan and Lukas and his daughters Maria and Barbara. The *Angel of the Annunciation* on the back

ALBRECHT DÜRER
Nativity (1503)
Lime panel; 61" × 49 1/2".
Not signed or dated, but datable
to 1503 through facts known about
the Paumgartners, the donors shown
in the painting.

of the St. Eustace wing, corresponding to the *Madonna of the Annunciation* on the back of the St. George wing, has disappeared, along with the predella panels; the presence of all these parts in the original work is documented by early copies of the altarpiece. In 1613 the triptych was given to Duke Maximilian I, and came to the Alte Pinakothek from the royal collection in 1836.

On his return from his first study trip to Italy, Dürer must have found himself in a very complicated psychological state in his native Nürnberg. Having studied his art over long years of devoted travel — first in Flanders, the Rhineland, Alsace and Basel, then in Venice and perhaps Lombardy — and having long been famous at least in the field of woodcut and engraving, he had just set up a studio and was beginning to receive the commissions for altarpieces and polyptychs that his old master, Michael Wolgemuth, was no longer able to carry out. These commissions, calling for patient hard work on the artisan level, kept Dürer tied to local tradition. At the same time, he had come back to Germany full of experience and loaded with drawings, his own and those of others, which were connected with the very different art world of Italy. Over these he must have meditated at length, racking his brains by himself or in heated discussions with Jacopo de' Barbari, who had been established in Nürnberg since 1500, on problems of perspective and the proportions of the human body. He was convinced that the Italians possessed the secret of the latter, but did not want to share it with him. At the very time that he was executing the panels for the *Paumgartner Altarpiece,* he was making one preliminary drawing after another for the famous engraving of *Original Sin,* which he was to publish in 1504, with the proud Latin inscription: "Made by Albrecht Dürer of Nürnberg." This would perhaps explain the fact that the results of his first Venetian experience are slow to become evident and appear fully only in the *Adoration of the Magi* (Uffizi), which was painted on the eve of his departure for his second journey beyond the Alps.

In the context of German painting of the time — even including the works of a forceful artist like Hans Holbein the Elder — the *Paumgartner Nativity* still stands out as a great innovation, especially in the structure of the composition. Similar compositions, obliquely disposed in depth, had already appeared in 15th-century Franconian painting, in competition with the more generally accepted frontal type, of Flemish inspiration. Yet what is new and remarkable about this work is the great care taken by the artist in the construction of the perspective. Aside from the existence of two vanishing points — very close to each other, however, with one serving for the building on the right and the other for the one on the left — it is almost an exact perspective that defines the space of the courtyard. There the Madonna and St. Joseph kneel before the Infant Jesus, while shepherds come in from the background, and the ox and the ass (right) and two old men (left) look on from the sides. A wooden lean-to and further back a robust arch cross the scene horizontally and slow down the perspective recession into the distance; they create a pause, as if to shape the space as a layering of masses in depth. Dürer has certainly caught the substance of Italian geometric spatiality, but he refuses to reduce his relationship with plastic mass

ALBRECHT DÜRER
St. George and *St. Eustace*
Lime panels; 61 3/4″ × 24″ each.
The St. George is held to be, with some doubt, a portrait of Stephan Paumgartner; the St. Eustace, a portrait of Lukas Paumgartner. Not signed or dated, but datable to 1503 through historical evidence, although some scholars consider these panels to be earlier than the *Nativity,* and datable to 1498.

to a purely mathematical relation of volume and space. Thus he opposes a full-bodied naturalism to the idealism of Italian painting, and his own profound vision of human suffering to the Italians' serene conception of a humanity made up of demigods living in a suitably harmonious world. In this way he achieves a solemn dignity, but at the cost of imposing a heavy moral burden on his bucolic personages. This gives meaning to the sense of urgent and compressed vitality in the clumsy attitude of St. Joseph, in the ponderous figure of the Madonna and in the rustic gait of the shepherds, as well as in the cutting of the plants clinging to the top of the ruined wall.

What is disturbing in the picture is the presence of all those minute donors and of the group of equally minute angels who are raising up the Infant Jesus. All out of scale, these little figures create a distracting agitation in the otherwise calm dignity of the composition. As for the figures in the wings, *St. George* and *St. Eustace* (page 38), so Italianizing in the concern with the proportion and the weightiness of the bodies, they are indeed most decorous. But the persistence in the contours of a linear vibration coming from the Gothic, ends by making the figures appear somewhat embarrassed in their pressing search for formal balance.

ALBRECHT DÜRER. *Self-Portrait in a Fur Coat.*
Dürer must have painted this *Self-Portrait* in the early months of 1500, some time before his birthday, which was on May 21. This would explain why the inscription in the background gives his age as 28 rather than 29. The solemn style and the broad, quiet forms show, however, that the painting must have been taken up again and largely retouched by the master himself in the early 1520's, after his visit to the Low Countries. For it is at that time that his portraiture acquired a new grandeur and power, accompanied by a greater density in color. The inscription, intended to consecrate this image of himself — which is based on the iconographic type of the Redeemer in benediction — must also belong to this second moment. Even if the first version of the painting, given the frontality of the scheme, aimed at the same general effect, it is certain that the definitive solemn and religious aspect is the work of the later repainting. In Dürer's later work, in fact, meditation on the spiritual essence of things — and in this case reflection on art as a gift of God and thus on the sacred character of the artist's function — prevails over the vitality and the intuition of reality that had been at the basis of Dürer's youthful work.

ALBRECHT DÜRER. *Lamentation over the Dead Christ.* p. 42
On stylistic grounds — and because it is known that the wife of the donor died before 1500 — it is possible to date this picture in the late fifteenth century. The composition is anticipated in Dürer's *Lamentation* woodcut in the *Great Passion* series, although the artist has here developed a more complex composition. He has discarded a centralized composition in order to achieve greater breadth, pathos and dramatic movement. In addition, he has avoided the isolation of the figure of the Madonna, which brought a harsh void into the formal structure of the woodcut, and has arranged the entire group of figures in a disciplined pyramid — a scheme of Italian origin — culminating in the figure of St. John. The expressive gesticulation of the

40

ALBRECHT DÜRER
Self-Portrait in a Fur Coat
Lime panel; 26 1/4″ × 19 1/4″.
Signed and dated on the left: "AD 1500."
On the right an inscription in Latin states that the artist painted himself at the age of 28. Monogram, date and inscription appear to have been repainted, but X-ray examination shows that they are authentic. Dating: 1500 and circa 1521–25.

figures in the print is replaced here by more ritualized attitudes and gestures, and only one old woman in the background still gives vent to her despair with a dramatic raising of her hands. The image of the Madonna, formerly stiff and solitary, is now the center of the whole group, tenderly surrounded by her friends as she wrings her hands in meek resignation. Bringing the lessons of Italian art to maturity, through long meditation, the artist arrived at a more complex structure in which the sense of harsh solitude is replaced by an expression of intense feeling that is, however, resolved in a choral composition.

ALBRECHT DÜRER. *Lucretia.*   *p. 44*

The idea for this picture goes back to two drawings of 1508 — one of the whole figure, the other of an arm — a date that is a decade earlier than the execution of the painting. This chronology gives proof of Dürer's deeply meditative temperament. Most art critics have been rather cold to this work, which was probably inspired by some Venetian nude, as it seems too concerned with maintaining the figure's equilibrium and getting the proportions of the human body right, at the expense of the drama of the event. Wölfflin, for instance, observes that in the original drawing Dürer reveals that his real interest is in the body as a living organism and that in the painting he is even more detached from the tragedy of the subject. In reality, the apparent coldness and the unquestionable intellectualism of Dürer's conception serve the artist's quest for a monumental expression of moral rigor. Thus the chastest nude in the history of art is born: a nude whose firmly contoured sculptural quality excludes any feeling of carnality. It should be noted that the loincloth is a bit of 17th-century repainting.

ALBRECHT DÜRER. *The Four Apostles.*   *p. 45*

The title of the painting has been universally accepted even though the fourth of the group of saints — John, Peter, Paul and Mark — was not an Apostle. In the artist's original intention the two groups would have flanked a panel of the Madonna, to make up a *Sacred Conversation.* He set to work in 1523 on a figure of St. Philip that was subsequently transformed into a St. Paul. After the town council declared in favor of the Reformation in 1525, it became impossible to show a painting of the Madonna in Nürnberg and Dürer gave up the idea of painting the central panel. Instead, he presented the two wings to the council, after having added long inscriptions of quotations from the Epistles of Peter, John and Paul and from the Gospel of St. Mark.

The texts cited, in German, warned against false prophets, against hypocritical rebels who pose as servants of God but in reality love pleasure and sin and are the very ones who sack houses and rape women, and against Scribes and Pharisees who pontificate in the schools and sponge off widows. From the contents of these quotations it is easy to deduce that Dürer intended to incite the city officials against the sects of "left-wing reformers" no less than against the Papists. Dürer substantially adopted the position of Luther and the influential men of the city, with whom he had ties of friendship and work, and was against the "communistic" interpretations of the Reformation that had led during those years to bloody tumults in the towns and to the

ALBRECHT DÜRER
Lamentation over the Dead Christ
Pine panel; 59 1/2″ × 47 1/2″.
Below on the left are the portraits of the goldsmith, Albrecht Glimm, and his two sons; on the right, his wife, Margreth Holtzmann and a daughter. At the sides are the coats of arms of the two families.

ALBRECHT DÜRER
Lucretia
Lime panel; 66 1/4″ × 29 1/4″.
Monogrammed AD and dated 1518.

Peasants' War in the countryside. This attitude should not be attributed only to an instinct for preserving his own social position. In view of the rigorous morality expressed in Dürer's work, it can be imagined that he viewed the mixture of religious with economic and social motives as a dangerous corruption of the Faith equal to — though in the opposite direction from — that caused by the trafficking of the Papist clergy.

Despite the travail of its creation, *The Four Apostles* is perhaps the greatest masterpiece of all Dürer's work, as well as the synthesis of all his experience as an artist. In the disposition of the figures, there is an echo here of Venetian painting, while the clarity of the plastic form recalls Italy in the broader sense. Equally evident are the taste for luminous surfaces, which is of Flem-

ALBRECHT DÜRER
The Four Apostles
Lime panels; 7′ 3/4″ × 2′6″ each.
Monogrammed AD and dated 1526.

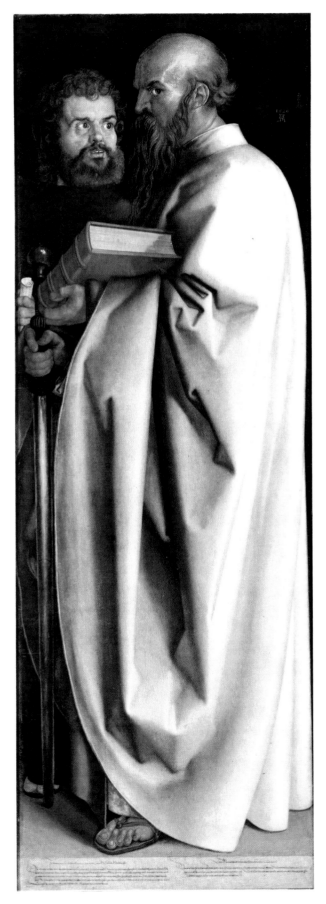

HANS BALDUNG called GRIEN
Schwäbisch-Gmünd circa 1480 —
Strasbourg 1545
Nativity
Pine panel; 41 3/4" × 28".
Monogrammed and dated 1520.

HANS SÜSS VON KULMBACH
Kulmbach 1476 — Nürnberg 1522
*Portrait of the Margrave Casimir
of Brandenburg*
(monogrammed and dated 1511).
Lime panel; 17" × 12 1/2".
The inscription, in German, gives the
name of the subject and his age, 30.

ish origin, and the fierce energy of the brushwork, which is nourished by the experience of a century of German art. But the proud, forceful sentiment that inspires the work leads to such a firm synthesis of opposites and to such imperious monumentality that no real comparisons can be found. The character of strenuous defenders of the purity of the Faith, which the artist attributed to the four superb Apostles, is expressed in terms of pure pictorial language. The ideal of the dignity and strength of man as a participant in divinity and in nature is exalted here in an ideal of struggle against, or rather unshakable resistance to, evil.

HANS SÜSS VON KULMBACH. *Portrait of the Margrave Casimir of Brandenburg.*

This notable painter, a native of Kulmbach in Upper Franconia, formed his style in Nürnberg when the influence of the Venetian Jacopo de' Barbari, resident there about 1500, was in the ascendant. Subsequently he worked with Dürer and became his closest collaborator. He was not immune, however, to the fascination of Altdorfer and the "romantic" atmosphere of the Danube School. Often with felicitous results, Süss combined the strength of Dürer's draftsmanship and plastic form with the warm color derived from Venice, and the results are at least tangent to those of the Danube painters. This fine portrait is painted with a sureness and a fullness of organization reminiscent of Dürer, and at the same time it is warm in color and has broad freedom of execution.

HANS BALDUNG (GRIEN). *Nativity.*

An Alsatian, Hans Baldung called Grien, after having learned his trade in some studio in busy Strasbourg, was Dürer's pupil from 1503 to 1505. Successively he worked in various places, including Strasbourg and Freiburg in Breisgau. Starting from a firm hold on reality, acquired as a follower of Dürer, Baldung arrived — through the use of singular enamel-like color and mysterious reflections — at his own "magic realist" vision. This vision has its most direct expression in the series, mainly of drawings and engravings, on witches and the dance of death. But in the religious subjects as well, as in this *Nativity* — preceded by the altarpiece of the same subject in the Cathedral of Freiburg (1516) — an aura of magic is felt. The space that opens up in the representation of the "hovel" is immense with respect to the size of the figures. On the other hand, the lunar light radiating from the Infant Jesus has its fantastic counterpoint in the mysterious aureole in the sky on the left and in the flash of the distant angel, beyond the doorway, to the right, lighting up the shepherds and the herd. Thus an earthbound rather than soaring effect is achieved; and this is tied to a peasant conception of faith, in which reverence for the sacred mystery is combined with a superstitious fear of what lies behind the appearance of things. In this atmosphere of magic astonishment, the ox and the ass may also be conscious participants in the act of adoration. It is possible for all to share in the mystery, because mystery is at the bottom of things and is the soul of nature.

HANS BALDUNG (GRIEN). *Prudence* and *Music.* p. 49

Sensuality in these two allegorical nudes exists solely in the eyes of the viewer; it does not stem from the artist. Baldung openly enjoys the discovery

of animality in man — an animality that is also a spontaneous and elemental manifestation of those magic forces that he discerns beneath the appearance of things. Variously interpreted as Science and Music or Vanity and Music, the two figures more probably represent Prudence (with the mirror, the serpent and the deer), as symbol of the melancholy and saturnine temperament, and Music, as symbol of the phlegmatic and sensual temperament. If this is so, the theme of the panels would be in perfect agreement with the lyric content of the two images. Tension animates the solid fleshiness of Prudence, whereas relaxation and sweet abandon define the firm sculptural form of Music. Together, they seem to state, in poetic metaphor, that the spirit of man is conditioned by the magic power of the stars. We know that Baldung was in agreement with Luther, and he perhaps used this way to express poetically, under the sign of "magic awe," the Protestant concept of predestination.

HANS BALDUNG called GRIEN
Prudence and *Music*
Pine panels; 32 3/4″ × 14 1/4″ each.
Both monogrammed, the *Prudence*
dated 1529.

LUCAS CRANACH THE ELDER. *Crucifixion.* p. 50

p. 50

One of the earliest known works of the master, it shows not only the influence of Dürer's graphics but also, in the unusual emphasis on perspective, a knowledge of Michael Pacher and the more warmly colored early works of Pacher's pupil, Marx Reichlich. Cranach, who was born in Kronach in Upper Franconia, is known to have been in Vienna around 1502–3 and may have passed through the Tyrol. The spontaneous and monumental simplicity of this composition reveals a spiritual affinity with the young Dürer.

The traditional frontal disposition of Christ on the cross is given up, and the cross, seen foreshortened from the side, penetrates into the background and by itself establishes space for the landscape view. In the left-hand corner, the cross of one of the thieves is similarly foreshortened. In opposition to the third cross, seen in front view, it forcefully marks out a measurable, square section of space, which the screen of trees to the rear distinguishes from, but also connects with, the open space of the background landscape. But the landscape is not merely space, it is primarily a study of nature, sympathetically observed. Note the evident emotion expressed in the rendering of the faint rustle of wind in the tall willow and the majestic oak, or the pale blue luminosity of the snowy Alps on the horizon, behind the brownish hills and cliffs carpeted with green. This light then affects the figures, creating a mysterious radiance in the yellow, deep blue and red of the sorrowing spectators' garments, and in the bloody and livid flesh of the crucified. Thus a complete fraternity between figure and landscape is created. And the spiritual harmony of man and nature is expressed, in measuredly romantic terms, in this and other early works of Cranach.

LUCAS CRANACH THE ELDER
Portrait of Geiler von Kaisersberg
(circa 1520–30)
Beech panel; 11 3/4″ × 9″.

LUCAS CRANACH THE ELDER
Kronach 1472 — Weimar 1553
Crucifixion (dated 1503)
Pine panel; 54 1/4″ × 39″.

LUCAS CRANACH THE ELDER. *Portrait of Geiler von Kaisersberg.* This is a posthumous portrait of the famous Strasbourg humanist and preacher, who lived from 1443 to 1510. The style of the painting suggests to some scholars a date around 1521 and to others around 1526–30, but in any case a date after the subject's death. The model was probably the woodcut frontispiece of Kaisersberg's *Annotations,* printed at Strasbourg in 1522. In this portrait — as in more famous examples, in several versions, of Luther and Catherine von Bora, of Melanchthon and Dr. Scheuring — a nervous, almost "Mannerist" line serves to render acutely observed physical details as well as tormented moral qualities. It has the "decadent" and escapist attitude of a generation that had intensely lived and suffered through the crisis of the age of humanism and the Reformation.

51

LUCAS CRANACH THE ELDER. *Lucretia.*

Although the artist's monogram and the date, 1524, appear to have been added later, a stylistic study of the painting substantially confirms their authenticity. The body covered with a drapery in the early 17th century (removed in a modern cleaning), this *Lucretia* once hung opposite Dürer's painting of the same subject in the private gallery of the kings of Bavaria. The contrast, even without the false drapery, could not be more significant. Compared to the austere morality of Dürer's *Lucretia* (see page 44), here a spiritual uneasiness is created by recourse to Gothic tradition, as in the crossed legs, and by the crackling linear tension of the contours and the studied, winsomeness of the pose. These features are accompanied by a sensual charge that later in the shop production of the artist's sons, Lucas the Younger and Hans, ultimately fell into ambiguous elegance or ponderous suggestiveness. The most felicitous phase of Cranach's busy activity is the "youthful" period before 1520 (actually late with respect to the painter's age), especially the beginning years from 1501–2 up to 1508, when he went to the Netherlands and absorbed the Flemish "Roman style." In that brief first moment he laid the foundations for what would later be called, especially after Altdorfer's contribution, the Danube School.

LUCAS CRANACH THE YOUNGER. *Venus and Cupid.*

Lucas Cranach the Elder's considerable production of female nudes — Venuses, Lucretias, nymphs, etc. — included a few masterpieces and a long series of commercial replicas to meet the demand of the market. His son continued this production in a highly pleasing though mannered style. The present painting is perhaps one of the best.

MATTHIAS GRÜNEWALD. *Mocking of Christ.* p. 55

First documented as being in Seligenstadt am Main in 1500, often resident in Aschaffenburg, Matthias Grünewald was perhaps a native of Würzburg. He died in Halle, after having spent the last years of his life in Frankfurt. The name of Grünewald by which the artist is famous comes to us from Sandrart's biography of 1675. His other two names — Neithardt-Gothardt — were discovered in documents in archives and are certainly authentic. Once Grünewald was made the champion of pure German art as against the humanism and Italian sympathies of Dürer, but critics are now beginning to recognize Flemish and Leonardesque influences on his work. It is nevertheless true that an exceptional "expressionist" charge makes this great artist a symbol of one of the most marked and frequently recurring aspects of German art.

This painting, which apparently comes from the Carmelite church in Frankfurt, bears the date of December 23, 1503. Although the date is a later addition, it was probably copied from the original, where it must have been painted on the frame or at the bottom of the panel, which has been cut down. The date corresponds to the year of Apollonia von Kronberg's death, and the picture, probably part of a memorial to her, was executed immediately afterwards. The painting is accordingly the master's earliest known work. In the pitiless characterization of the faces of the thugs and in the violence of their actions, the work is related to some very prevalent features of

Left:
LUCAS CRANACH THE ELDER
Lucretia (probable date 1524)
Lime panel; 6′4 1/4″ × 2′5 1/2″.

Right:
LUCAS CRANACH THE YOUNGER
Wittenberg 1515 — Weimar 1586
Venus and Cupid
Lime panel; 6′5 1/4″ × 2′11″.

German painting in the first half of the 15th century. On the other hand, it avoids any connection with the closer currents of the so-called Late Gothic Baroque of the end of the century. Despite these elements, there is nothing archaic in the work to affect its modern conception. For instance, there is no longer any trace of the fragmented, episodic composition of 15th-century work that so displeased Dürer. Instead, there is a close-knit, unbreakable unity. A wheeling movement, turning off-center on the seated Christ, passes from the figure who has raised his hand to aim a blow to the one in the foreground pulling on the rope. Thus, the entire composition is involved in a kind of eddying motion. The harsh realism of the images and the description of the violence are absorbed by the rhythm of an incessant and irresistible movement, and the real is transformed into something supremely unreal.

Vivid and contrasting in hue, the color is altogether extraordinarily fused and impregnated with light in a way that, although very different from the Venetian, must still be defined as tonal. This chromatic density cancels the limits of the still "Gothic" contours and gives the painting atmospheric unity. From the point of view of art, the expressive power of this work lies precisely in the contrast between truth and unreality. The initial drawing represents the "truthful" side, while the color — in its animation of the forms and in its resolution of a lively variety of hues in a new unity — represents the transfiguring element. We thus find already present in this painting, which is on the threshold of Grünewald's better known activity, those two opposed features of a pitiless realism and an exalted visionary spirit. It is a most original vision with its roots deep in certain mystic currents of the period, currents that called for a live participation in the Passion and at the same time its transformation into a visionary conception.

MATTHIAS GRÜNEWALD. *The Disputation of St. Erasmus and St. Maurice.* pp. 56–57

This work was commissioned by Cardinal Albrecht of Hohenzollern, Prince-Archbishop of Mainz, for the Collegiate Church of SS. Maurice and Mary Magdalene at Halle, a church that he had founded in 1518 and consecrated in 1523. The cardinal, who was a friend of Erasmus of Rotterdam, belonged among the "doves" of the Catholic party and sought a compromise with Luther. The disputation shown here — between St. Erasmus, bishop and pastor of souls as well as the namesake of the Dutch philosopher, and the armed champion of the faith, St. Maurice — alludes in fact to the conflict between the "doves" and the "hawks" of that era. Although the painter obviously did not attempt to translate the arguments of that disputation into pictorial terms, he nevertheless felt their seriousness and significance. And perhaps, as a sympathizer with the extremists of the Reformation and with the peasant uprisings, Grünewald felt that, despite the hopes of the cardinal, the outbreak of an open and bitter struggle was near.

The painting is pervaded by a heavy and secretly dramatic atmosphere, which finds its figurative expression in the turgid tonalism of the color. Saturated with light, it is laid on in deep tones and builds up by itself the powerful figures, in turn saturating the deep, dark space with tone. What is com-

54

MATTHIAS GRÜNEWALD
(MATTHIAS NEITHARDT–GOTHARDT
Würzburg circa 1470 (?) — Halle 1528
Mocking of Christ (dated probably 1503)
Pine panel; 43″ × 28 3/4″.

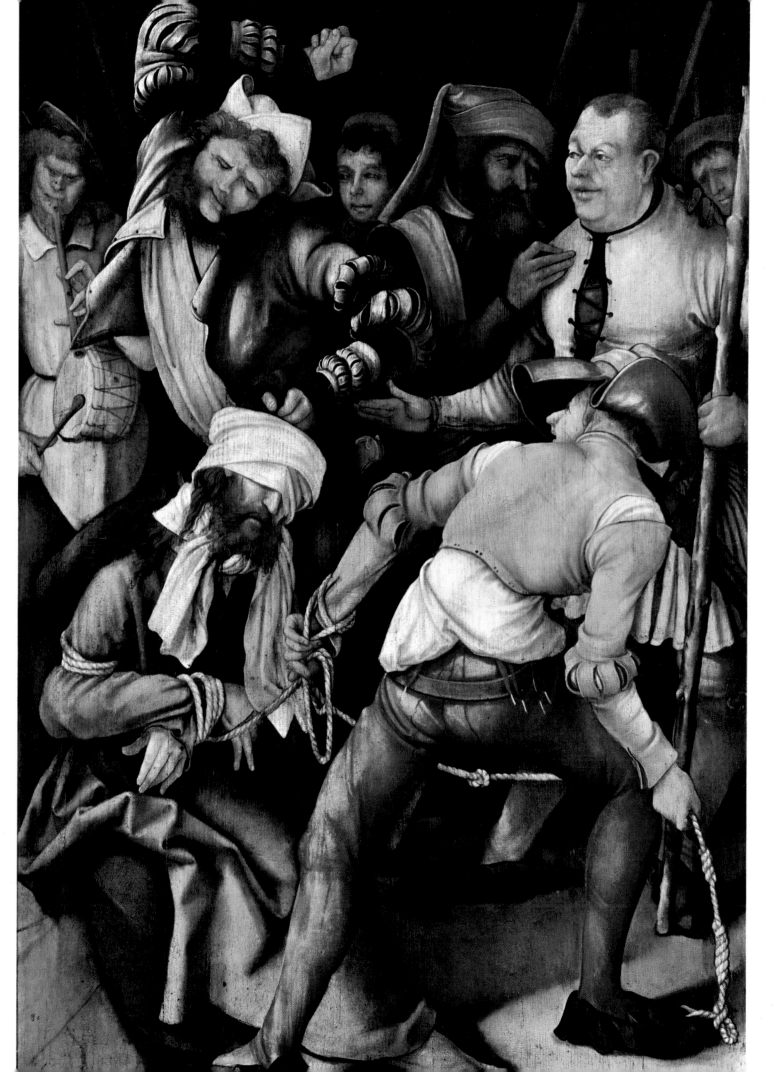

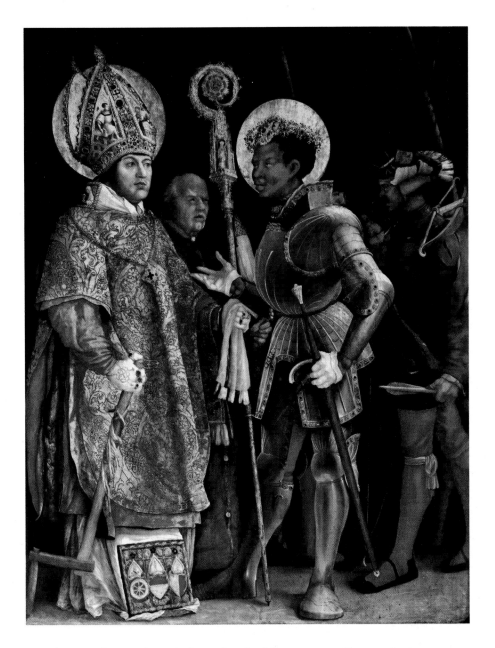

posed as a chromatic unit is a chord of hues concealing explosive power, and from it comes a fantastic and unreal illumination in which the visionary spirit of the artist broods. It is a grandiose work, comparable in quality and depth of speculative and moral commitment to Albrecht Dürer's *The Four Apostles* (page 45).

HANS LEONHARD SCHAEUFELEIN. *The Agony in the Garden.*

p. 58

Probably born in Nürnberg, Schaeufelein as a youth must have frequented Dürer's studio, as compositional motives from Dürer's work often recur in his pictures. He cannot, however, be considered a real and proper student of the great Franconian painter. For some time he was also active as an engraver, and at Augsburg, where he was staying in 1512, he participated in the great woodcut projects promoted by the Emperor Maximilian. In 1515

MATTHIAS GRÜNEWALD
*The Disputation of St. Erasmus and
St. Maurice* (circa 1523)
Lime panel; 7'5" × 5'9 1/4".
Left: Detail

57

HANS LEONHARD SCHAEUFELEIN
Nürnberg circa 1480 — Nördlingen circa
1540
The Agony in the Garden
Lime panel; 20″ × 15 1/4″.
Monogrammed and dated 1516.

he established himself in the Swabian city of Nördlingen, where he was to live until his death. The Renaissance atmosphere and the orientation toward Italy of the imperial city of Augsburg — also the home of the outstanding painter, Hans Burgkmair, who reflected the influence of Venice — had its effect on the unpretentious painting of Schaeufelein. This is seen in the compositional balance, the studied foreshortening and the intense warmth of color in this painting.

ALBRECHT ALTDORFER. *St. George in the Forest.*

The minute figure of the cavalier saint, who is about to slay the dragon, is a mere pretext for the creation of the earliest and most fascinating landscape in German painting. The drawing is so precise that it would virtually be possible to count the leaves of the giant oaks and the luxuriant beech trees

ALBRECHT ALTDORFER
Amberg or Ratisbon?
circa 1478 — Ratisbon 1538
St. George in the Forest
Parchment on lime panel; 11″ × 8 3/4″.
Monogrammed and dated 1510.

in the thick woods. But besides being clear, the drawing is strong and every detail is charged with energy. The multiplication of details and the insistence in the coloring on highly dense and luminescent green tones create the image of a thick, live forest in its totality. It is a landscape made up of living reality but also one fantastically and romantically animated by the strong pulse and the primal force of nature. So much freedom of the imagination, outside the conventional schemes, was the result of a new demand for such little pictures on the part of art lovers and collectors who were participants in Renaissance civilization.

ALBRECHT ALTDORFER. *The Birth of the Virgin.*
Perhaps born at Amberg in the Palatinate, Altdorfer established himself in and became a citizen of Ratisbon — where his father, an obscure painter called Ulrich, had lived — and he thus became the true founder of the Danube School. A knowledge of the works of Pacher and his circle must have contributed to Altdorfer's development. Two apparently contradictory tendencies dwell together in the artist: close adherence to the natural aspect of things, down to the smallest details; and an unbridled fantasy and imagination. On closer inspection, these qualities are seen to be complementary, and are held together by a feeling for nature that cannot be defined other than by the term romantic. The perspective technique learned from Pacher is seen here again in this *Birth of the Virgin*. But to amplify the sense of space beyond any rational perspective system, the painter attracts our eye deep within the vast cathedral. Against all the rules, the space is seen from two viewpoints, one below the lower margin of the picture — so that Joachim's legs are cut off — and the other at the level of the canopy on the left. And the wonderful, novel invention of the flight of angels embracing no less than three pilasters, with a sweep like a bombastic hymn, also helps to enlarge the space. The spatial intuition — not construction! — identifies itself with the intuition of the fantastic light, and elevates the quiet description of the figures and their actions to the sphere of an exalted vision.

ALBRECHT ALTDORFER. *View of the Danube Valley.* *p. 62*
This is a real landscape, identifiable as lying near Ratisbon, with the castle of Wörth and the Scheuchenberg in the background, and thus it is unquestionably the earliest true landscape in German painting. Even though a real view, it is also classical in the studied framing of the composition, with two "wings" of trees in the foreground and the balanced perspective of the distances, showing the wooded hill on the right and on the left the counterweight of the mountain by the river. Furthermore, the energy of the drawing and the fervor of the color transfigure this real view into a fantastic vision, making it a vigorous expression of the tranquil and majestic power of nature. The Danube School of the 16th century showed the influence of Altdorfer's fresh and intense landscapes. And on the verge of the 17th century a different but related imaginative affection for nature unfolded in the painting of Adam Elsheimer.

ALBRECHT ALTDORFER. *The Battle of Alexander.* *pp. 63–65*
Commonly called the *Alexanderschlacht* in German, it represents Alexander's battle against Darius on the river Issus, and bears the bulletins, in

ALBRECHT ALTDORFER
The Birth of the Virgin (circa 1525)
Pine panel; 55 1/2" × 51 1/2".
Probably from Ratisbon, where an old copy exists.

ALBRECHT ALTDORFER
View of the Danube Valley
Parchment on beech panel; 11 3/4″ × 8 1/2″.
Monogrammed. Datable circa 1520–25.

Latin and German, of the losses inflicted on the enemy and those suffered. It was one of a series of historical paintings commissioned by Duke Wilhelm IV of Bavaria for his summer house, the Lusthaus, in Munich.

A favorite with the public visiting the Alte Pinakothek, the painting is admired for the virtuosity with which a vast number of figures has been included in a relatively small space. Indeed, the little figures of the combatants could actually be counted one by one throughout the distant view. The technical skill of the artist is undeniable, but no less noteworthy is his imagination. Fundamentally not so different from his other paintings, this work is enhanced by the multiplication of the figures and by the minute details of the landscape, so that it becomes a grandiose vision. Thus in the open, flashing light of the wonderful picture, the battle expands into a cosmic event in which the sun and the moon, the clouds and the air take part.

It is worth recalling that there is an unmistakable reference to this painting — perhaps through some copy or variant — in *The Suicide of Saul* (1562) by the great Flemish painter, Pieter Bruegel. In that work the Israelites and the Philistines in battle are similarly shown as hosts of minute, many-colored figures, though the spirit of the whole is entirely different.

ALBRECHT ALTDORFER
The Battle of Alexander
Lime panel; 62 1/4″ × 47 1/4″.
Monogrammed and dated 1529.
On pages 64–65: Detail.

ALEXANDER·M·DARIVM·VLT·SVPERAT
CÆSIS·IN·ACIE·PERSAR·:PEDIT·:CM·EQVIT
VERO·XM·INTERFECTIS·MATRE·QVOQVE
CONIVGE·LIBERIS·DARII·REG·CVM·M·HAVD
AMPLIVS·EQVITIB·:FVGA·DILAPSI·CAPTIS·

ADAM ELSHEIMER. *Flight into Egypt.*

This masterpiece cannot be understood without a review of the astonishing career of the artist, who was educated in Frankfurt by the German Uffenbach and by Flemish masters such as Coninxloo and the various Valckenborchs. From Uffenbach he inherited his attachment to German tradition, to which he then gave his own interpretation through his knowledge of Altdorfer and the painters of the Danube School; from the others he assimilated an echo of Bruegel's astonishment over the grandeur of nature. But in early youth Elsheimer went to Venice and in 1600 to Rome, where he fell in with Caravaggio and his followers and was also influenced by Annibale Carracci. He thus succeeded, as Longhi evocatively put it, "in reflectively filtering in his little Roman studio the flashing chiaroscuro of Caravaggio, which was all nature, and the solemn masses of the Carraccis' landscape, which was all history." The key to his unity and coherence, despite the complexity of his works, is to be sought in the frankly idyllic inspiration of the artist, an inspiration that is supremely affirmed in this little picture. It is a romantic nocturne in which the figures and the landscape lose their material individuality to live in the astonished silence of a moonlit night.

ADAM ELSHEIMER
Frankfurt 1578 — Rome 1610
Flight into Egypt
Copper; 12 1/4″ × 16 1/4″.
Signed and dated "1609, Rome."

FLANDERS

JAN GOSSAERT (MABUSE). *Danae.*

The style of Jan Gossaert, called Mabuse, is of fundamental importance in understanding the spread of the so-called Italian manner to Flanders at the beginning of the 16th century. Other artists had adopted some of the techniques developed in the Italian Renaissance, yet those techniques served merely as the basis for what were predominantly formalistic or repetitious exercises. Mabuse, however, possessed an exceptional ability to revivify these techniques with his own imagination. The influence of Florentine and Venetian perspective is evident in his work. But a tight formal synthesis characterizes, almost incises, the figures, which are further defined by rich, brilliant color in the Flemish tradition.

This *Danae* is particularly indicative of Gossaert's style, not only for its high quality but also for its iconography, which is typical of the artist. In fact, Mabuse, following the Italian example, introduced the practice of representing mythological subjects to Flanders, and along with masters like van Cleve, Quinten Metsys and other minor artists, painted scenes taken from Lucretius. The intensity of the contrast between the firm columnar architecture and the almost brute vitality of the half nude body struck by the shower of golden light gives such force to the brilliant play between emotional tension and solid centralized construction as to make this little panel perhaps the artist's masterpiece.

LUCAS VAN LEYDEN. *Madonna and Child, Mary Magdalene and Donor.* *p. 70*

Lucas van Leyden, one of the greatest engravers of the 16th century, still presents serious problems of attribution and dating to students of his work in painting. He was the pupil of his father, who was not an outstanding artist; but Gossaert and Dürer are considered to have had a determining influence on his development. Often, however, an insistence on such "influences" impairs judgment and blurs an exact historical evaluation of an artist.

The work in question is one of Lucas van Leyden's few dated paintings and accordingly is fundamental to a reconstruction of the artist's stylistic development. It was executed a year after Lucas met Dürer in Leyden, a meeting that unquestionably coincided with the moment in which the Dutch master was most like Dürer in style. In fact, iconographic models that can be traced to the great German artist are present here. Lucas' interest in Venetian painting may also derive from Dürer; and this was an interest that assumed a personal and original form in his later works. Certainly in these years, as the present work attests, there is an accentuated dwelling on sharp description and precision of line. Compared to works like the *Portrait of a Man* in London or the *Brazen Serpent* in Amsterdam, in this *Madonna* the graphic element seems to be fundamental in defining the complex compositional re-

68

JAN GOSSAERT called MABUSE
Maubeuge in Hainault 1478 — Antwerp 1534
Danae
Oil on panel; 44 3/4″ × 37 1/2″.
Signed and dated: "Joannes Malbodius
Pingebat 1527"
Danae, daughter of the King of Argus,
is loved by Jupiter, who comes to her
in a shower of gold. From the
Royal Gallery of Munich.

lationships. Although the color range here is always rich and clear, it stands out less than the intensely taut color fields of the later works. Similarly, the figures are closely related to and almost absorbed into the complex description of the fine landscape, thus avoiding the tense spatial relationships that are already to be found in the *Last Judgment,* executed only four years later.

JOOS VAN CLEVE.   *Death of the Virgin.*
For many years van Cleve was known only as the Master of the Death of the Virgin, after the famous altarpiece dated 1515, which is now in the Wallraf-Richartz Museum of Cologne, and this splendid painting in Munich. Indeed, his short catalogue of pictures has been reconstructed entirely around these two fundamental works. Perhaps a native of the Lower Rhineland (his name would suggest that he came from Cleves), he probably lived in Genoa — two of his paintings are preserved in that city — with Philip of Cleves, the lord of Ravensteyen, from 1501 to 1506. Having moved to

LUCAS VAN LEYDEN
(LUCAS HUIGHENSZ or HUGENS–
ZOOM)
Leyden 1489? — Leyden circa 1533
Madonna and Child, Mary Magdalene and Donor (dated 1522)
Oil on panel; 19 3/4″ × 26 3/4″.
As Van Mander states, it was in the Emperor Rudolph II's collection, from which it passed to Maximilian I's Kammergalerie.

70

Antwerp, he was associated with Joachim Patinir, and subsequently he worked in France and England.

A strongly theatrical layout characterizes the master's work, and in particular this *Death of the Virgin*. In a stage-like setting of marked perspective effect, the figures run about feverishly, creating a syncopated but highly decorative rhythm throughout the composition. In the same way, the characterization of the faces is substantially unified in a single collective emotional physiognomy. In this dynamic emphasis there is an echo of the great personalities in German painting of the late 15th century. But beyond the door (right), which is decorated with the festoons and busts dear to the Italianizing Flemish tradition, and beyond the window (left), the space extends in accordance with an accentuated perspective division. Thus, the walls of the room close off a portion of space as in the "appointed place" or stage of a mystery play.

CORNELIS VAN DALEM.   *Landscape.*

Joachim Patinir's entourage still represents one of the most fascinating problems in 16th-century Flemish art. The master was the originator of a type of landscape whose antecedents are sought in Bosch and Gerard David. However, he knew how to give his landscapes classical system, that is, a clearly rational structure worked out in a minutely descriptive, ably thought out and modulated synthesis. These features are found in every one of the painters more or less directly connected with Patinir, including Cornelis van Dalem. In his works the accentuated modular development of the composition is accompanied by a notable ability to create a luminous and subtle play of color.

PIETER BRUEGEL THE ELDER.   *The Land of Cockayne.*

The Land of Plenty, with all its delights, welcomes the representatives of

CORNELIS VAN DALEM
Active from 1535 to 1576
Landscape (1564)
Oil on panel; 40 1/2″ × 50 1/4″.
Monogrammed and dated. It belonged to
the Hugo Bruckmann collection in Munich.

PIETER BRUEGEL THE ELDER
Bruegel? 1530? — Brussels 1569
The Land of Cockayne (1567)
Oil on panel; 20 1/2″ × 30 3/4″.
Dated and signed. In the inventories of Hradčany Castle in Prague from 1621 to 1648, then disappeared in the Swedish conquest. It reappeared at Vevey at the end of the 19th century, completely repainted, and was acquired by Dr. Henry Rossier for five francs. In 1901 he resold it after restoration, to the German collector, Kaufmann, for 10,000 francs. When his collection was auctioned off in 1917, the painting was acquired by the Alte Pinakothek.

the three estates — peasant, cleric, soldier — to the shade of the tree of plenty. Special treatment is reserved for the nobleman in armor resting under a shed covered with pies. In the background a fifth figure enters Cockayne in the approved way, that is by having dug a tunnel through the mountain of buckwheat. The tidbits promenade about and grow like trees. The roast chicken goes and puts itself on the plate, the hog moves around already partly sliced and the boiled egg strolls across the foreground. It is an irresistibly savory representation — one that, through complex symbols, is ready to follow the course of transformation into morality so typical of Bruegel. But this vividly fantastic narrative is also supported by a complex structure, the radiating construction centering on the foreshortened tree. Some scholars have seen this as typical of the "anti-classicism" of the master, but in fact it goes back to his study of Raphael's method, interpreted with free and irrepressible brilliance.

73

PETER PAUL RUBENS. *The Artist and His First Wife, Isabella Brandt.*
It appears that this portrait was painted by Rubens in the same year as his marriage to Isabella Brandt, daughter of one of the best-known humanists in Antwerp, Jan Brandt. The symbolic bower of honeysuckle, the affectionate placing of the right hands and the somewhat ceremonial and official clothes all suggest a commemorative work. It celebrates an emotional event, however, and the "pose" of the two figures may even be intended as good-natured domestic irony.

This is the first of the family groups in which the artist took pleasure in portraying his splendid and serene home life and the two beautiful women who were successively his wives: Isabella Brandt and her niece Helena Fourment. Already rich and famous, the 32-year-old painter shortly before had concluded his first great Italian experience. His enthusiastic rereading of the great Venetian masters of the 16th century is reflected in the accentuated plasticity of the forms and in the Veronesan lights and shades of the color. His free-flowing inventiveness in form, however, has the stamp of exalted visual felicity and total ethical serenity, characteristics that mark Rubens' style at its highest.

PETER PAUL RUBENS. *Drunken Silenus.*
When it reached its full maturity, the triumphant vitality of Rubens' pictorial

language nullified the classical structure and balance that still ruled in his preceding works. This *Silenus* still shows the survival of accentuated symmetry and the classical St. Andrew's Cross scheme, but the composition has been brilliantly transformed. The grotesque procession centers on the tottering figure of Silenus, who is drawn along, close pressed by now vividly illuminated, now unexpectedly shadowed bacchants, satyrs and lively country folk. Below the broken-off vine branches and hemmed in by bounding animals and children, a female satyr suckles her little monsters. In the steep foreground she appears to rise from the ripe earth, and her vitality is tempered by a luminous wave of bluish and pinkish whites fortified by nacreous pulsations. Rubens' sensuality — that of a rich Flemish bourgeois — was a never-ending stimulus to his imagination, but without losing any of its felicity here it unexpectedly achieves a high formal synthesis.

PETER PAUL RUBENS.   *Rape of the Daughters of Leucippus.*

This painting is of prime importance in understanding how Rubens overcame modular classical structure "from within." The great wheel made up of extended elements balanced against one another is in wonderfully calculated compositional equilibrium. Without disruption, the two female nudes stand out perfectly, each showing the side concealed in the other, so that they are entirely complementary. But this highly measured modulation is countered by an emotional vision, that of a cultivated yet brutal humanity. The opulent Venetian nudes become mystical in their overgrown sensuality, as they twist and clutch in the grip of the Dioscuri, between the terrible, plunging horses. Isolated from the vortex of the event, a squinting cupid, attached like a wasp to the flank of the horse, smiles knowingly. In the background the landscape extends serenely into the vast distance. In this contrast, which is emphasized by the low horizon line, the foreground is thrown into even greater emotional relief, almost against the light, and is relieved and balanced only by the variation of the color.

PETER PAUL RUBENS.   *Battle of the Amazons.*   p. 78

It appears that Rubens was inspired to paint this work by Titian's *Battle of Cadore*. Yet Titian's great canvas, which was part of the decoration of the Gran Sala in the Palazzo Ducale, had already been destroyed in a fire when the master visited Venice, so Rubens probably knew the work only from Fontana's engraving of the scene. Unlike the Venetian painting, the dramatic climax here is centered on the arched bridge, which accentuates the composition's whirling torsion, flung far into the distant reaches of the river. In the group on the bridge the memory of Leonardo's *Battle* is also evident, but here the exultant knot of bodies is loosened and explodes into a panicked flux of limbs, reeds and water. The diaphanous bodies of the fallen warrior-maidens, lying on the bank or carried away by the current of the river, are as luminous as water creatures. They squirm in impossible contortions in the balanced play of contrasts and rhythmic cadences, which are paired in this work. After the emotional impact of a first view, these are seen to be a regular part of an exactly calculated pulsation, in an organization that

PETER PAUL RUBENS
Rape of the Daughters of Leucippus
(circa 1618)
Oil on panel; 7'3 1/2" × 6'10 1/4".
From the Düsseldorf Gallery.
According to the Greek myth, the daughters of Leucippus, betrothed to the sons of Aphareus, were ravished by the Dioscuri in the course of a fight.

77

otherwise might seem chaotic. In sum, a sort of visionary metaphor is created, in which the sense of death and the horror of the slaughter are nullified.

PETER PAUL RUBENS. *Lion Hunt.*

This celebrated painting is very much alive in modern history through its reinterpretation by Delacroix. The symmetrical correspondences seem to accentuate the leaping movements of the men and the beasts. Each detail is charged with a tension that is immediately transformed into an active sounding of the space. The narration is so powerfully synthesized as to appear elliptical where the opposite process brings out the opulence of lively, detailed representation. The figures form a dramatic knot, isolated in the midst of an otherwise deserted space, thus indicating that the memory of Leonardo's *Battle* is not a learned citation but a precise and aware cultural choice. According to some scholars, Van Dyck painted the figures of the hunters, while Rubens merely retouched them. However, certain traits of

PETER PAUL RUBENS
Battle of the Amazons (circa 1618)
Oil on panel; 47 3/4″ × 65 1/4″.
It belonged to the Düsseldorf Gallery. The dating was obtained by stylistic evidence and from a letter Rubens wrote to Pieter van Veen on January 23, 1619, in which he states that he had recently finished the painting.

these figures are typical of Rubens alone and do not belong to the repertory of his great pupil.

PETER PAUL RUBENS. *Fall of the Rebel Angels.*   *p. 80*

With the *Large Last Judgment* and the *Small Last Judgment,* both in the Alte Pinakothek, this work is witness to Rubens' complex train of thought on a subject of great structural intricacy. It is obvious that Michelangelo's great example was still alive and necessary to Rubens. In the *Large Last Judgment* the composition is still conventional, exactly divided into geometric portions marked by a heightened differentiation in light and color. The second work on this theme shows a more powerful pulsation of the tangle of anatomies, and in its system of steep, inclined planes it is already a prelude to the fulminating Day of Wrath of the *Fall of the Rebel Angels.* Having chosen a single moment of the final drama, the most terrible moment for the damned, the painter hurls the mass of streaming bodies, dazzled by the archangel's shield (top left), into the infernal gulf. Shapes and features are canceled in the red, almost monochromatic glare that deforms and consumes them. It is the drama of sinful humanity in the mind of the most visionary, human and felicitous genius of the century. Grotesque, deforming physical terror is transformed into a gigantic blaze, a delirious

PETER PAUL RUBENS
Lion Hunt (1616)
Oil on panel; 8'2" × 12'3 3/4".
Painted for Duke Maximilian of Bavaria, it belonged to the Royal Gallery of Munich. The identification of this work, on the basis of a letter the artist wrote to Sir Dudley Carleton, is questioned by Burckhardt. His view is that the *Hunt* painted for Maximilian was the one formerly at Schleissheim Castle, which was subsequently destroyed in a fire at Bordeaux in 1870.

79

maelstrom in which every element has its own grandiose vitality, and objective dimensions are turned into enormous space in a total vision.

PETER PAUL RUBENS. *Apotheosis of Henry IV and the Regency
Given to Marie de' Medici*

In all Rubens' paintings for Marie de Medici, as in the poem of the Cavalier
Marino, mythology with its events and heroes are incarnated in the lives of
Henry IV and his Queen. Here the King (left) is welcomed to Olympus by
Jupiter and the genius of Time, while Bellona and Minerva weep for his
death. The Queen (right) is seated on a throne between Minerva and Prudence, who are there to inspire and console her. Meanwhile, the spirit of
Good Government offers Marie France and the other lands of her realm.
But the opulence and the "baroque" conceit of the symbols, their commemorative hypocrisy, are overcome by the fervid orchestration of the fantastic and splendid narrative. The small size of the composition concentrates
the brushwork, bringing out the slightest emphasis, without falling into an
excessively synthesized illusionism.

Compared to other sketches by Rubens, these in the Alte Pinakothek are
more finished, even if they do not always correspond exactly to the large
final versions done for the Luxembourg Palace in Paris (now in the
Louvre). The relationship between these small works and the large canvases
may offer a solution of the problem concerning the function of Rubens'
sketches. In the sketches, in fact, the master primarily measures off the space
and calibrates the figures and the settings — at times also the color relation-

ships — with an ease that the large-sized compositions would not permit. The fact that the sketches were not memory aids for students — whose part in executing the great canvases is usually exaggerated — is shown not only by the exceptionally high quality of the painting, but also by the numerous variations, from which unexpectedly brilliant solutions often emerge.

PETER PAUL RUBENS. *Landscape with Rainbow.*
The dating of Rubens' landscapes is particularly problematical. As far as this work and the following one are concerned, there might be a clue in the stylistic affinities with the large landscape at the National Gallery of London. In that canvas, Steen, the country house bought by the painter in 1635, is shown.

Rubens was familiar from childhood with this genre of representation, a tradition that was very much alive in Antwerp. He broadened his experience in this respect during his stay in Rome, where very likely he frequented the

PETER PAUL RUBENS
Landscape with Rainbow (after 1635?)
Oil on panel; 37 1/4″ × 49 1/4″.
Belonged to the Düsseldorf Gallery.

studios of Bril and Elsheimer; and after his return to Flanders he had as a friend and collaborator Jan Bruegel, called "Velvet Bruegel," who was one of the greatest landscape painters of the time. But the master's imagination does not fall into even remotely derivative patterns. In comparison to his friend's minute descriptiveness, the awesome immensity of Rubens' landscapes sums up a moment of feeling. The light is always cast as a dramatic means of measuring space, and develops the narrative of the picture with an unusual, probing sensitivity. It completely portrays the dying day of the countryside, reflected and sinking into the woods, and the light returning from the plain to the cloud-hung sky. This poetic interpretation of life is the means by which the artist, identifying himself with natural things, perhaps more than ever before attains a total humanity.

PETER PAUL RUBENS. *Landscape with Cows.*
As in the preceding work, the high viewpoint — recalling Philips de Koninck and Ruisdael — permits the representation of a vast sweep of landscape. The wing made by the woods opens like an enormous loop, in which the light reverberates and turns. It enfolds and makes the view fluid, identifies the sky with the trees and relates these to the figures, which are rendered with a narrative exactitude that is also full of feeling.

PETER PAUL RUBENS
Landscape with Cows (after 1635?)
Oil on panel; 32″ × 41 3/4″.
From the Royal Gallery of Munich.

83

PETER PAUL RUBENS. *Massacre of the Innocents.*
Almost certainly painted during the years when the Marie de' Medici cycle
was taking shape, this work recalls the sketch for the *Apotheosis of Henry
IV* (also in the Alte Pinakothek; see page 81). Except for a perceptible displacement of the viewpoint, it repeats the relationship of architecture and
space and the placing of some of the figures. Here the dramatic pulse of the
composition is strongly accentuated. On the right, in a tumultuous flow, the
figures fall about, stretched and splayed dramatically with their faces con-
torted, in a way that directly recalls the most terrible episodes in the *Lion
Hunt* (see page 79). The tensely arched, opulent female figure in the center
sets the rhythm for the entire scene but at the same time creates a pause and
makes the action easier to grasp.

PETER PAUL RUBENS. *Helena Fourment with Her Son Francis.*
Rubens was greatly saddened by the death of Isabella Brandt, his first wife,
in 1626. Four years after this tragic event, he took the 16-year-old Helena
Fourment, a niece of Isabella's, as his second wife. Helena's beauty became
almost the essence of Rubens' feminine ideal. His portraits of her that have
come down to us number no less than nineteen. In these the painter also
liked to portray the children of both marriages, as if this youthful concert
of childhood and maternity were for him an eternal song of happiness and

PETER PAUL RUBENS
Massacre of the Innocents (circa 1621)
Oil on panel; 6'6 1/4" × 9'11".
It belonged to Cardinal Richelieu's
collection. In 1706 it entered the
Kurfürstl Galerie.

PETER PAUL RUBENS
Helena Fourment with Her Son Francis
(circa 1635)
Oil on panel; 57″ × 40″.
At first smaller — the composition stopped
at the knees of the female figure and half
way up the small balustrade column on the
extreme right — it was subsequently enlarged by Rubens himself. It belonged to
the Munich Gallery.

joyful fullness of life. This portrait and the one in the Louvre are among
the most sumptuous of the series. Its pomp is somewhat amused and know-
ing, as often seen in the "familial" works of the Flemish master. This is ex-
emplified in the feathered hat on the nude child, which gives an unexpectedly colorful effect that enhances its tender irony. And it brings to mind
the splendid "Rothschild Portrait," in which the painter and Helena are
strolling with their first-born, and in which the joyous family activity is in
contrast with the gorgeous opulence of their clothes. It is a contrast in which
the happiest artist of his century, the idolized genius and great diplomat,
states and immortalizes the deep truth of his affections.

JACOB JORDAENS. *Satyr at the Peasant's House.*

Of the various interpretations of Aesop's fable by Jordaens, the present work and the version acquired in 1940 by the Royal Museum of Brussels are undoubtedly the most famous. The painting is harsh, with strong contrasts in light. The faces are characterized to the point that they become types, and the emphasis on detailed description becomes a fabulous view of reality. In contrast to Rubens, Jordaens defines his pictorial surfaces with great, almost stubborn exactitude, and encloses his compositions in the strongly geometrical and modular systems of the Flemish tradition. More than in his splendid portraits, the master's highest creativity is found in canvases like this. Tradition finds here a new creative dimension in the enchanted, de-

JACOB JORDAENS
Antwerp 1593 — Antwerp 1678
Satyr at the Peasant's House
(circa 1620)
Oil on panel transferred to canvas;
5′8″ × 6′8″. It belonged to the
Düsseldorf Gallery. The subject is one
of the best known of Aesop's Fables.

ANTHONY VAN DYCK
Antwerp 1599 — London 1641
Self-Portrait (1621–22)
Oil on canvas; 31 3/4" × 27 1/4".
From the Düsseldorf Gallery.

tached observation of the things represented. And this is very different from the so-called "realism" that is often attributed to the Flemish master.

ANTHONY VAN DYCK. *Self-Portrait.*

The 22-year-old painter depicted here already had a considerable body of work behind him. Now having his own studio and his own pupils, he had already been Rubens' favorite assistant and a court painter in England. About this time, he went to Italy, where — despite his considerable earlier work — his full maturity began. He established himself in Genoa and became the official portrait painter of the great Genoese families. From Genoa Van Dyck traveled to Florence, Rome and Venice. Although some Venetian

87

ANTHONY VAN DYCK
Portrait of a Gentleman (1624)
Oil on canvas; 6'11 1/4" × 4'6 1/4".
Acquired in 1698 by Maximilian II Emanuel
from the collection of Gisbert van Ceulen.
In all likelihood it is the portrait of Charles
Alexander von Croy; its pendant, a portrait
probably representing Countess von Croy,
from the same collection, is also in the
Alte Pinakothek.

influence had already come to him through Rubens, his direct experience in the city itself — of Tintoretto, Veronese and above all Titian — was fundamental to the development of his pictorial language. His famous *Notebook* (London, British Museum) reveals that his study of Titian was not merely scholarly interest, but a means of self-clarification and historical investigation. In particular, he admires and lists all of Titian's portraits. Indeed, this *Self-Portrait* in Munich, which was painted exactly during the months of his visit to Venice, clearly shows his preference.

Note the relationship between the figure and the background, and the monochrome passage of the costume interrupted by the slight opening of the collar. The oblique fullness of the pose is already typical of Van Dyck, as is the almost cantankerous tilt of the head — a subtly theatrical attitude in which the acute characterization of the face plays an important part.

ANTHONY VAN DYCK. *Portrait of a Gentleman.*
This is a noble example of the full-length portraits typical of Van Dyck's mature manner, portraits that were to have so much importance in the development of the grand tradition of English portraiture. Here the subject is set forth as in a eulogy, and the basic features of pride and nobility are represented in a splendid unity of pose, drapery and background. In all of Van Dyck's masterpieces, however, these external and documentary features are magnificently resolved in a system of equilibrium that may well be called ethical. They become true and proper portraits of inner nobility, in which the external pomp is only the mirror and the account of an absolutely conscious privilege. For this reason, Van Dyck's great portraits have a particular stamp, and in them the splendid iconography and the penetrating psychological perception have an equal function.

A red parasol, an enormous black mantle or a piece of scarlet lace — found in other portraits of his — are merely emblems of the official personage, but they have exactly the same weight as the glance and the portentous carriage of the subject. Here, against a deliberately artificial architectural background, the subject assumes a broadly open pose and balances it with an intensely calm expression.

ANTHONY VAN DYCK. *Deposition.*
As shown by the date, 1634, this work was painted during a brief stay in Antwerp, when the artist returned to Flanders on family business. The religious theme is another confirmation that the picture could not have been done in England, where Van Dyck had been established since 1632, and where such Roman Catholic subjects were not allowed to be represented.

The composition is one of the most spectacular in Van Dyck's entire repertory. It makes up a tight pyramid that appears to collapse and spread under the accentuated weight of the figures and the drapery, but is held together internally by the miraculous equilibrium composed of varying directions

ANTHONY VAN DYCK
Deposition (1634)
Oil on panel; 43" × 58 3/4".
Initialed "A.V.D.F." above on the
right, and dated 1634. It belonged to
the Düsseldorf Gallery.

and deformations. The splendid passage between the head of Mary and that of Christ connects with the exaggerated expanse of the nude body. This baroque representation thus becomes a blazing description of sorrow. For this reason it was necessary to include the tempestuous arrival on the scene of the angels, and the grotesque and melting compassion of the cherubim, in a convulsed landscape in which the deformed light is a measure of the mood. A suggestion of the pathos of Titian's *Deposition* in the Louvre may be discerned, despite the difference of the Venetian master's intense restraint.

89

ANONYMOUS FLEMISH ARTIST. *Family Portrait.*

Of high quality, this work is an example of a genre for which 17th-century Dutch and Flemish painting was celebrated: the family portrait. Even though it does not possess the emblematic austerity of portraits by Cornelis de Vos, nor the narrative emphasis of those by Jordaens (not to speak of some of the masterpieces of Rubens and Van Dyck), this canvas appears to include all the standard features of the genre. The matron, heavily sheathed in lace, is the only figure in the group to hold a dignified, almost emblematic, pose, as if weighed down by the effort it cost her to produce all those children. The shrewd-looking, florid-faced father, on the other hand, proudly shows the offspring in question. The children, meanwhile, are engaged in their favorite pastimes. The girls — one of them dressed for the country — play with a basket of fruit. Showing humanistic tendencies, the two boys on the left are engaged in drawing and conversation. A less seriously inclined son, in the center, is playing with a dog. In the background may be seen the family's villa in the country.

ANONYMOUS FLEMISH ARTIST
Circa 1630
Family Portrait
Oil on canvas; 7'3 1/2" × 9'9".
It belonged to the Munich Gallery.

HOLLAND

ESAIAS VAN DE VELDE
Amsterdam circa 1591 —
The Hague 1630
Skaters on the Moat by the Walls
Panel; 11 1/4″ × 19 3/4″.
Signed in lower left: "E. V. VELDE 1618."
From the von Pfalz-Zweibrücken collection. A relatively youthful work, it was executed soon after the artist's arrival at The Hague. There, until his premature death, he was very active, serving also as court painter to Prince Maurice and Prince Frederick Henry.

ESAIAS VAN DE VELDE. *Skaters on the Moat by the Walls.*

Van de Velde's interpretation of the "winter landscape," a genre with a long and flourishing tradition in the Netherlands, is notably different from those of his contemporaries. The narrative, which is given a "real" setting at the edge of a town, is set forth in an explicitly organic manner. The thin little profiled figures are carefully arranged in a movement paralleling that of the setting: the wall turning in a semicircle and the progressively receding grassy banks on the opposite side. The interest with which the artist handles the basic theme of this genre is new. The violent contrast between black and white in Bruegel's treatment of ice has become, in the hands of his imitators, a facile play of pleasing but obvious effects. Here it seems that van de Velde seeks instead a solution in unitary tonality, which is crude and almost cruel in its stinging harshness. The skeletal branches and the stiffened fronds, the frozen walls and the human specks diminishing and ever more evanescent in the rarefied atmosphere — all recede rapidly and silently toward the distant background. There a pale evocation of trees and houses prevents the meeting at the horizon of the gray whiteness of the frozen ground and the dull luminescence of the pitiless sky.

ADRIAEN BROUWER. *Interior with Four Peasants.*   *p. 94*

The masterful perspective of this painting alone would be enough to suggest the name of Brouwer. The play of geometrical forms — to which all the elements of the background are largely reduced — matches the placing of the figures in an oblique rectangle, with the upright of the chair in the foreground serving as its forward corner. Although this carefully composed rhythmic equilibrium indicates that Brouwer himself did this painting, at least one critic has placed it among the many imitations that crowd the catalogue of the artist's work.

There are some incidental passages of less intense sincerity, especially in the figures, and there is an unusual horizontal broadening of the composition, accompanied by a relaxation in some secondary and not very stimulating episodes. All this perhaps suggests that the artist was less committed to this work, rather than that he was not the true author.

FRANS HALS. *Portrait of Willem Croes.*   *p. 95*

The portrait is a scanty bust-length, immobile in its frontal symmetry, and the face has an ordinary good-humored air and a commonplace expression. The deliberately modest image goes well with the execution, which as always with the painter is pared down to the essentials. Thus the evocative power

of the brushwork, which is broad, fluent, imbued with color and light and overwhelmingly modern, stands out all the more. And all the more evident is the explosive vitality of this master who knows how to evoke so much in a face beyond its physical features and expression. He creates a "reality" that goes beyond the individual portrayed and even beyond the historical moment and the social and geographical situations, in order to acquire a higher human validity. And this is achieved with expressive means that could be of our own times.

REMBRANDT VAN RIJN. *Self-Portrait as a Young Man.*   *p. 96*
More than a hundred self-portraits of the artist exist, and those showing him in youth are particularly numerous. In fact, Rembrandt does not distinguish himself from his work and readily uses his own image throughout his long career — either to record moments, situations or events in his own life, or for more complex reasons. Among those reasons may be research in pictorial method concerning color effects, chiaroscuro and composition;

ADRIAEN BROUWER
Oudenaarde 1605 or 1606 — Antwerp 1638
Interior with Four Peasants
Panel; 17" × 22 3/4".
From the Kurfürstliche Kunstkammer.
Probably a work of the artist's late years in Antwerp. Knuttel (1962) has suggested that it is a later imitation.

FRANS HALS
Antwerp circa 1580 — Haarlem 1666
Portrait of Willem Croes
Panel; 18 1/2" × 14 1/2".
Detail.
Signed at lower left with the artist's monogram. Acquired in 1906 from the van Stock collection in Haarlem. The artist's chronology is not easy to establish, but this work certainly belongs to his splendid final period.

REMBRANDT VAN RIJN
Leyden 1606 — Amsterdam 1669
Self-Portrait as a Young Man
Panel, 6″ × 5″.
Signed with the artist's monogram and
dated 1629. From the
Sachs-Coburg-Gotha family foundation.

studies in psychological expression; or notes on settings or on genres, such as the Oriental, the beggar, etc.

This image of Rembrandt at the age of 23 is unquestionably a combined experiment in form and psychology. A large part of the face is in shadow, as if to make one forget the eyes that are scrutinizing themselves and their own meaning. The summary indication of the bust, which is just enlivened by the contrast between the white collar and the dark garment, and the slightly oblique position, which gives an elegant profile, proclaim the artist's voluntary renunciation of facile effects in order to concentrate his attention on the real subject: the hair. The sprouting locks of hair seem to move by themselves, while lighter, vibrant strands (Rembrandt scratched them into the surface with the wooden end of the brush, it appears) in the dark mass leave only a large area of cheek in the light. Strong and sure, built up with broad, rapid, structural brushstrokes, the image stands out forcefully against the subtle nuances of the background. It has the genuineness of a live and eloquent presence, which further increases the frankly romantic fascination of this self-confident youthful portrayal.

REMBRANDT VAN RIJN. *The Raising of the Cross.*   *pp. 98–99*
In the large concave space pervaded by heavy oppressive darkness, the diagonal motive of the cross with the already stiffening body rises abruptly. Like an unexpected spurt of flame, it flares up, with its pitiless light revealing every detail of its tragic burden. While the thick, subdued crowd of bystanders is lost in the dark shadow, the lateral light source barely brings out some of the more important episodes in the narrative. In a continuation of the main diagonal motive, the light slides along the soldier's armor, creating reflections reminiscent of Van Dyck, and centers on the spectator in the blue cap. This stupendous and incongruous figure is a self-portrait that the artist has inserted into the composition. (See detail on page 99.) The fulcrum of the whole work, it is set off against the neutral, almost monochrome, background of the other figures, by the wonderful blue of the costume. This specific presence, representing real life, stands in contrast with the impersonal. distracted, chilled and mute actors in the rest of the sacred drama.

REMBRANDT VAN RIJN. *The Descent from the Cross.*   *p. 100*
Painted the same year as the preceding work, with the same vertical development and also with the presence of the artist (the blue figure on the ladder), the second episode in the cycle further accentuates the noble silence and abstract remoteness of the representation. The great precedent established by Rubens in his painting of the same subject in the Cathedral of Antwerp (1613) is often cited in connection with this work. This may be done, if at all, to emphasize the contrasts. In fact, the Rubens work — a tumultuous, crowded, diagonal landslide of luminous drapery, soft flesh, ecstatic faces and blond hair against the ground of the white sheet — is truly the most antithetical image it is possible to imagine to this silent and reserved episode of lofty piety. Here the tapering pyramid formed by the main group, which is struck by powerful light toward the top, is broadened at the base by figures that are just discernible in the indeterminate sepia mono-

chrome. Also present but indistinct are the details of the setting, motionless against the broad dark surface of a lifeless sky. Again, there is no pulsation and no note of color in the rarefied concave space in which the bloodied cross rises like a broken arrow.

Another standard comparison, with Rembrandt's 1633 engraving of this subject, is just as arbitrary, because of the great diversity of the two works. It is not the difference in the means of expression nor the variations, which in any case are secondary, but rather the differing significance and tone of the engraving that count. The parts that are only suggested in the painting are exactly described in the engraving, while the importance of the painting's main group is brought out by the light, whereas in the print this is done by increasing its size.

REMBRANDT VAN RIJN. *Entombment.*   *p. 100*

Commissioned in 1636 and completed in 1639, this work shows the last act of the Passion tragedy. Set in a hallucinatory atmosphere, thick with heavy shadow, the episodes are picked out by light from three different sources.

Above:
REMBRANDT VAN RIJN
The Raising of the Cross
Canvas rounded at the top; 39 3/4″ × 28 1/4″.
This and the following four paintings come from the Düsseldorf Gallery.
With the *Descent from the Cross,* it was commissioned in 1632 by the Prince Regent of Orange, through his secretary, Constantin Huyghens. Both works were completed in the following year. These, and the others subsequently commissioned in 1636 and 1646 (see following illustrations), make up a real "Passion cycle" whose function from the beginning, however, was not intended to be religious. It should be emphasized that neither the patron nor the artist ever thought of placing them in any church, despite the subjects and the round-topped format taken from 16th-century Italian altarpieces.

Right:
Detail, showing the artist's self-portrait.

These make the points of a triangle that the artist has inserted obliquely and broken on the inside. It suggests a diminishing perspective toward the background and the upper part of the picture, and at the same time symbolically expresses a yearning towards a transcendental hope. In fact that is the meaning taken on by the wide opening in the shining sky, with the distant, immaterial suggestion of the crowd on Golgotha and the now empty crosses. A very different power of evocation is seen in the torch on the left, whose light pitilessly exposes the body, the tomb and the mourners, isolating the main episode in a magic aura of reddish gleams. The space occupied by this scene is defined by figures seen in front view, profile and from the back, and making a slow ovoid rhythm. Finally, the tilted lantern in the right foreground feebly lights the group of the Three Marys, composed in a short pyramid and connected with the lateral figures at Christ's feet. Apparently complex and fragmented, the entire work is unified through its refined solutions in lighting and composition, and once again the artist succeeds in creating — on a canvas of relatively modest size — a sense of limitless space, outside of time and history.

100

Left:
REMBRANDT VAN RIJN
The Descent from the Cross
Canvas rounded at the top; 36 1/4″ × 27 1/4″, real size, without additions, 35″ × 25 1/2″. Bears the false signature: "C. rembrant f." Painted in 1633. The subject was often repeated by Rembrandt and his followers.

Above:
REMBRANDT VAN RIJN
Entombment
Canvas rounded at the top; 36 1/2″ × 27″. Executed between 1636 and 1639. Some scholars assume that the painting in the University of Glasgow is the preliminary sketch for this work.

REMBRANDT VAN RIJN. *Resurrection.*

In a letter of January, 1639, Rembrandt wrote to his friend Constantin
Huyghens: "I have sought to express in these two pieces [in this and the
similar *Ascension,* which is not reproduced] the strongest movement possible, and this is the reason why I have been working on them for so long." A
burst of rotary motion seems to be created around the motive of the angel
and the smoking clouds that enfold it, and which have the value of an ex-
plosion of light within the picture itself. It is from this resplendent whirl-
wind that the light pours down, softly diffused on the bust of the risen Christ
(right) but striking in brief and fragmentary flashes on the entangled forms
of the soldiers and on the dumbfounded Marys below, to the right.

REMBRANDT VAN RIJN. *Adoration of the Shepherds.*

After eighteen years, the artist has taken up again the problems and inten-
tions involved in the preceding cycle of pictures and has given them a solution that is simpler perhaps, more immediate, but substantially similar.
With his little lantern, Joseph creates a warm hollow of golden gleams   101

around the newborn child, and the lighted circle he forms with Mary and the shepherds is isolated as an episode in itself. However, the feeble lantern in the upper left and the luminous cloth in the lower right include this grouping in a single path of light that crosses the picture diagonally. Around this axis unfolds the marvelous, mysteriously shadowed evocation of the stable, so real and warm, and the speechless, astonished spectators in the background, who have halted on the threshold. There is an immediate sincerity in each image and an intense, vibrant participation that transfigures everything. In the scanned rhythm of the perspective, diminishing toward the darkness of the background, beams and supports acquire the noble grandeur of an imposing building.

AERT VAN DER NEER. *Winter Landscape.*

The juxtaposition of this illustration and the following one — two solutions to the same problem that are at once similar and different — allows us to show the qualities of structure and composition that are essential to an understanding of 17th-century Dutch landscape painting. For the most part, such landscape painting is understood and explained in terms of its descriptive and naturalistic values, or it is interpreted in its psychological implications and the feelings it conveys. All these elements are present in these two pictures, but they are not enough to reveal their intrinsic truth.

Van der Neer, following the example of van de Velde, elaborates the two horizontal divisions of the landscape in broad, open and opposed curves. Above, in the broader part of the canvas, there is the circular movement of the slowly gathering clouds; below there are the curvilinear developments of the shores, the little figures, the bushes and the clumps of trees. The artist has a clear recollection of the preceding tradition's specific, inhabited landscape, and he is still attracted by the contrasting play of black and white in the "winter landscape." But one feels an aim toward unity, in the solid, reciprocal rhythms that connect all the elements of the composition in a broad, general harmony.

PHILIPS DE KONINCK. *Extensive Landscape.*

The horizontal division in this landscape by de Koninck follows more or less the same proportion as that of the preceding work. In the wake of van Goyen, especially, the artist has eliminated — or removed the significance — of any precisely descriptive elements. The water among the dunes strongly marks a diagonal path of light directed toward the background on the left. The swollen mass of the darker clouds above marks a corresponding but inverse movement. In this predetermined, solidly unified structure, the artist distributes the graduated planes of the surface and the areas of light and shade in rhythmic patterns. Yet the needs of the organized construction do not disturb in the slightest the extraordinary spell of this romantic fantasy, wrapped in a magic silence.

AERT DE GELDER. *The Jewish Bride.*   *p. 104*

The lesson of Rembrandt, learned by the artist when he was a boy in the by then elderly master's shop, is entirely evident in this painting, which belongs to de Gelder's own maturity. It is a lesson, however, that is obviously con-

AERT VAN DER NEER
Amsterdam 1603–4 — Amsterdam 1677
Winter Landscape
Panel; 9" × 13 1/4".
Signed. From the
Aschaffenburg Gallery.

PHILIPS DE KONINCK
Amsterdam 1619 — Amsterdam 1688
Extensive Landscape
Canvas; 52 1/2" × 65".
Acquired on the
Munich art market in 1927.

AERT DE GELDER
Dordrecht 1645 — Dordrecht 1727
The Jewish Bride (Esther Bedecked)
Canvas; 54 3/4″ × 64 1/4″.
Signed upper right (barely visible)
and dated 1684.
From the Mannheim Gallery.

fined to surface aspects: the subject, proportions, types, accompanying details and general disposition. What is lacking, with respect to Rembrandt's work (see especially the *Jewish Bride* in the Rijksmuseum, Amsterdam) is the exceptional, unitary intensity of the light, which here is broken up in the prominence of every single element. Also missing is the essential simplicity of the composition, which in this picture turns on the contrast between the main figures, shown knee-length in the left foreground, and the space to the right. This space contains suggestions of the milieu and the setting and establishes a three-dimensional effect. The significance of the whole representation lies in the rendering of a specific situation, solidly anchored to a moment and a meaning in reality.

JAN STEEN. *Lovesick Woman.*

Here we find almost an anthology of the narrative and compositional formulas of mid-17th-century Dutch painting, interpreted with conscious satisfaction but also with genuine enthusiasm. These are the play of light and shade in many variations; the fitting together of geometric elements; the perspective views of silent interiors; the masterful *trompe-l'œil* of woven wool and wicker; narrow openings to the side giving glimpses of the exterior; dense masses of one color (here going back to Flemish 15th-century tradition); and the predilection for still life, animals, handsome faces, the fresh sheen on silks or furs and thick glass or metal objects. All of this large repertory of different elements is unified by the cheerful atmosphere created through carefully directed lighting, by a sobriety underlying the richness of the representation and finally by the happy and instinctive participation of the artist in his own narrative.

JAN STEEN
Leyden 1626 — Leyden 1679
Lovesick Woman
Canvas; 24 1/4″ × 20 1/2″.
Signed on the letter, which bears a
verse in Dutch meaning: "No medicine
helps, if the pain is love."

GERARD TER BORCH. *Boy Picking Fleas from a Dog.*
This is a simple, direct genre scene, in which nevertheless there are some
cosmopolitan elements cited by scholars as typical of Ter Borch and result-
ing from his frequent travels abroad. In this case some recollection of Spanish painting, for instance of the contemporary Murillo, appears to emerge
in the contrast of the softly modeled form with the bare background, and in
the gentle melancholy that pervades the little figure of the boy and the sparse
details of the setting. The triangular composition favored by the artist,
which he usually prefers to employ frontally and symmetrically, is here displaced diagonally towards the interior, as clearly shown by the wooden
bench in front. From the corner of the bench up to the beginning of the part
in the child's hair, the main axis solidly supports the composition, which
slowly revolves around it, drawing the spectator's attention to the wonderful examples of still life on the left.

GERARD TER BORCH
Zwolle 1617 — Deventer 1681
Boy Picking Fleas from a Dog
Canvas transferred to panel; 12 3/4″ × 11″.
Signed lower left.
From the Mannheim Gallery.

GERARD TER BORCH. *The Letter*.

More typical of Ter Borch's figurative world than the preceding work is this group, which is inscribed within a triangle with impeccable precision. Its height, that is, the axis marked by the woman's figure, is displaced toward the right, as on the right the three figures in the narrative are graduated in depth. They are distracted and appear suspended in a void, despite the summary indication of a background and the more elaborate rendering of the foreground. There is an atmosphere of mute expectation, without a tremor, in the clarity of a cold, impersonal light that freezes every element it describes in a lovely refinement.

PIETER JANSSENS ELINGA. *Woman Reading*.   *p. 108*

This interior in part repeats Janssens Elinga's well-known *Empty Room* (Brockhaus collection, Lugano). It retains that work's light source on the left, with the precious pearliness and the vibrant nuances of its reflections, as well as the clear distribution of the geometric elements. The foreshort-

GABRIEL METSU
Leyden 1629 — Amsterdam 1667
The Bean-Feast
Canvas; 31″ × 38″.
Signed on the child's chair to the right.
From the Düsseldorf Gallery.

PIETER JANSSENS ELINGA
Active in the second half of
the 17th century in Amsterdam.
Woman Reading
Canvas; 29 1/2″ × 24 1/2″.
Acquired in 1791 from de Vigneux.

ened view in this scene seems more intimate and quiet, thanks to the reduced height and the inclusion of some evidence of human presence: the slippers, the apples in a bowl, the reflection in the mirror and — just as allusive and mute — the woman seen from the back, who is absorbed in reading. The faceless immobility of the figure emphasizes the pervasive presence of silence, which enfolds every object with an emotional intensity like that borne by the light in its dominant, sovereign and unifying role.

GABRIEL METSU. *The Bean-Feast*.

Poet of a happy and rich daily life, Gabriel Metsu derives from the composed and mirror-like reality of his master, Gerard Dou, a masterful assurance in the rendering of every form and every object represented. But like van Ostade and Jan Steen in their late works, he seems to be inspired rather by the crowded and boisterous compositions of contemporary Flemish painters. He borrows their concern with plastic effects and oblique lighting to the extent that in this little folk celebration he gives us almost an imitation of Jordaens' banquets, which were very well known in Holland through numerous replicas and imitations.

109

JACOB VAN RUISDAEL. *Landscape with Hill and Trees.*

Although it strikes a romantic note, this view of a rocky hill with the wind blowing its leafy masses is constructed on a framework of complicated structural coordinates. This is so complex as to represent one of the most explicit examples of the predetermined construction and organization always present in the work of the great landscape painter.

The separation of sky and land runs along a sinuous line dividing the surface of the panel almost in half, with the land swelling up on the left and the sky — in mathematical correspondence — fuller on the opposite side. All of the elements in the landscape have a sinuous development. Most evident and most insistent of all in this respect is the road, but it is also true of the contours of the trees, the trunks, the branches and the grassy and stony patches. The dense system of curves in opposition or correspondence is emphasized here and hidden there, as the light falls, in a continuous play of contrasts or rhythmic symmetry. This is not limited to the surface. Indeed, here we have a typical example of the "modeling in flexible masses" that is very often found in Ruisdael's landscapes. They are to be understood principally as structures in depth, made up of blocks, masses or planes arranged and balanced in accordance with strict criteria of space and volume.

MEINDERT HOBBEMA. *Landscape.*

A similar composition, divided into areas and modeled in gradated masses, is seen in this landscape by Ruisdael's pupil, Meindert Hobbema. Here, however, it reveals the mechanics of the structure, a preoccupation with illustrative aspects and a minutely analytical execution, such as are never found in the work of Hobbema's master. The slow, sinuous development of the wide road leading to the background is accompanied by the typical motive of the wings, composed of trees arranged in parallel succession according to a simple rhythm that clearly contrasts vertical and horizontal elements. The relaxed and peaceful image allows us readily to grasp the artist's pleasure in observing the natural features of the landscape; the movement and effects of light and shade in that landscape he notes with great delicacy of perception.

PAULUS POTTER. *Peasant Family with Domestic Animals.* p. 112

The descriptive aim of this little scene is apparent, with its careful attention even to the grotesque details of the setting and the figures. Potter was already justly famous during his brief life for his affectionate and exact observation of animals, and here the sheep and cattle have a predominant part in the picture. They fit into the framework of the composition and enhance the careful structure, so that their presence completes the pleasing atmosphere of bucolic tranquility.

JACOB VAN RUISDAEL
Haarlem 1628/29 — Haarlem 1682
Landscape with Hill and Trees
Panel; 27 3/4" × 36 1/4".
Signed lower center: "Ruisdael 16.7."
Inherited by Maximilian I, it was
given to the Gallery in 1825.

MEINDERT HOBBEMA
Amsterdam 1638 — Amsterdam 1709
Landscape
Panel; 20 1/2" × 25 1/2".
Acquired in 1792 from de Vigneux.
Signed lower right.

PAULUS POTTER
Enkhuizen 1625 — Amsterdam 1654
Peasant Family with Domestic Animals
Panel; 14 3/4″ × 11 1/2″.
Signed upper left and dated 1646.
From the Kassel Gallery, in an
exchange made in 1803.

PIETER SAENREDAM. *Interior of the Church of St. James, Utrecht.*
The foreshortened view of a Gothic choir, with a painstaking display of the
complex interrelationship of surfaces and ribbing, is a typical example of
the Dutch church interior as a genre. These impressive interiors, empty and
silent, vibrant with diffused atmospheric light, most obviously testify to the
compositional severity that underlies and affects the image — even in other
subjects — of 17th-century Dutch painting. More clearly than elsewhere, in
fact, the articulation of gigantic, bare architectural structures allows for
compositional solutions worked out in terms of the most varied rhythms.
These may function in terms of symmetry, correspondence, contrast, con-
vergence toward a central or lateral vanishing point, a high viewpoint or a
low one, and so on, making up a wealth of formulas that may be varied to
satisfy an almost unlimited range of the imagination.

PIETER SAENREDAM
Assendeft 1597 — Haarlem 1665
*Interior of the Church of
St. James, Utrecht*
Panel; 21 3/4″ × 18″.
From the Archiepiscopal
Gallery of Würzburg.
Among the memorial tablets hung on the
pillars, the first on the left bears the artist's
signature and the date of 1642. The little
figures seen in Saenredam's work are usu-
ally by Adriaen van Ostade or Pieter Post.
Sometimes they are later additions, prob-
ably executed during the course of the 18th
century.

JAN VAN HUYSUM. *Basket of Flowers.*

It has been correctly observed that this imitator of the specialists in floral still life was clearly influenced by the contemporary French painters, Monnoyer and Fontenay. If it is true, however, that van Huysum has carried the genre to a point of mechanical ability, in the wake of their example, he has not followed their more complex and varied representations but has stayed in the tradition of the elegant, sober prototypes of the Dutch and Flemish 15th century. These are immersed in a soft penumbra and enriched with the abundance of rare flowers, the variation of planes and the decorative rhythms added by generations of specialists in the course of the 17th century. Van Huysum, who was called their "Phoenix," carries on their consummate virtuoso ability, their camera-like precision and their wealth of color, yet adding his own typical marble-cool clarity.

114

JAN VAN HUYSUM
Amsterdam 1682 — Amsterdam 1749
Basket of Flowers
Panel; 15 1/4″ × 12 3/4″.
Signed lower right.
From the Hofgartengalerie, where it
was brought from Schleissheim in 1781.

ITALY

GIOTTO
(GIOTTO DI BONDONE)
Colle di Vespignano 1267? —
Florence 1337
Active between 1290 and 1300 in
Assisi, from 1302 to 1306 at Padua.
After 1310 works principally in
Florence, but also visits
Naples, Milan, etc.
Christ in Limbo (circa 1320–25)
Tempera on panel; 17 3/4″ × 17 1/4″.
Predella panel.
Acquired by Maximilian I of Hapsburg.

GIOTTO
Crucifixion (circa 1320–25)
Tempera on panel; 17 3/4″ × 17″. Predella
panel. Acquired by Maximilian I. The presence of St. Francis at the foot of the cross,
with the donors, suggests that the work was
probably executed for a Franciscan church,
perhaps S. Croce in Florence.

GIOTTO.   *Christ in Limbo* and *Crucifixion.*

These two little panels belong to an advanced phase in Giotto's career. Famous and widely celebrated after the completion of the fresco cycles in S. Francesco at Assisi and the Arena Chapel at Padua, Giotto at this time was directing a busy studio in Florence. Between 1318 and 1325 he also was working on the *St. John the Baptist* and the *St. John the Evangelist* scenes in the Peruzzi Chapel and the *St. Francis* scenes in the Bardi Chapel of S. Croce.

Relating these two works in the Alte Pinakothek (which also possesses the *Last Supper*) to other panels of the same size (*Adoration of the Magi,* New York, Metropolitan Museum; *Presentation in the Temple,* Boston, Gardner Museum; *Deposition,* Florence, Berenson collection; *Pentecost,* London, National Gallery) some art scholars have reconstructed the predella of one of the four polyptychs that Giotto painted for the chapels in S. Croce. Other, larger panels scattered among various museums are thought to belong to this work. Among the problems presented by this reconstruction there is the relatively small size of the chapels, which would mean either that the hypothetical polyptych was intended for another place, or that the panels come from more than one of the S. Croce works. The scholars do not agree on the question of Giotto's authorship; for some this is certain, while others ascribe the little paintings to studio assistants. In actuality the sureness of the compositional framework, which aims at a sober, compact effect, certainly comes from the master's own hand.

In the panel that represents *Christ in Limbo* — showing Christ drawing forth the righteous who were not baptized (Adam and Eve, Abraham, David, Solomon, etc.) — a large, faceted rock, in whose hollow the figures are crowded, occupies half the space. On the rock the damned are being tormented by demons, as Christ, accompanied by Dysmas, the Good Thief, whom he will also take to Paradise, helps Adam up by the hand. In the *Crucifixion,* where perhaps more of the execution was shop work, the gold ground takes the event out of its historical context and enhances the compact quality of the figures. These are compositionally connected below, but separate and almost counterpoised in the upper part of the picture. Christ on the cross is in the center; kneeling at his feet are St. Francis and two donors; to the right is St. John the Evangelist with Nicodemus and Joseph of Arimathea; to the left is the Virgin, who has collapsed heavily into the arms of the Three Marys.

FRA ANGELICO.   *SS. Cosmas and Damian before Lysias* and *Entombment.*   *pp. 118–19*

For the church of S. Marco, whose clear-cut construction by Michelozzo has been lost through successive alterations, Cosimo and Lorenzo de' Medici commissioned Fra Angelico in 1440 to execute a large altarpiece with predella for the high altar. The altarpiece represents the Madonna and Child enthroned between angels and saints, with the two miracle-working patron saints of the Medici family, Cosmas and Damian, in the foreground. It is now in the adjoining Museo di S. Marco, whereas the predella was dismembered and during the 19th century was scattered among various museums.

GUIDO DI PIETRO or FRA
GIOVANNI DA FIESOLE called
FRA ANGELICO
Vicchio 1387? — Rome 1455
At Foligno and Cortona around 1418. Subsequently active in Florence, where he begins the decoration of S. Marco in 1436; and in Rome from 1447 to 1449 and from 1454 to 1455.
SS. Cosmas and Damian before Lysias (1440–42)
Tempera on panel; 15″ × 18 1/2″. Predella panel. The other six panels are divided among the Alte Pinakothek, the Museo di S. Marco in Florence, the Louvre and the National Gallery in Dublin. Acquired on the Berlin art market in 1822.

The *Entombment* was in the center, while events in the lives of Cosmas and Damian, who had been martyred in Asia Minor and whose cult had become widespread both in the East and in the West, were depicted in six side panels. The legend of the two saints offered artists broad possibilities for descriptive scenes, since before their decapitation they had been subjected to various forms of torture, such as being scourged, crucified, shot with arrows and thrown, chained, into the sea.

In the first panel reproduced here, the two saints with their younger brothers Antimus, Leontinus and Euprepius stand before the proconsul Lysias, who asks them to sacrifice at the feet of the idol in the niche on the right. An intense and uniformly diffused light shines on the pink and white marble wall. A cultivated humanistic recollection of classical forms, the wall backs up the orderly arrangement of the figures, and in the repetition of the fluted columns gives rhythmic scansion to the subdivision of the figures into groups. The first (left) includes the two saints, side by side. Then follow the three younger brothers, who also have halos, as they, too, will be martyred. Next come Lysias, spreading his arms in an eloquent gesture, and the two counselors or priests. Finally there are the two soldiers in the foreground, who are placed in the last of the regular divisions of the space, corresponding to the space occupied by the foreshortened idol in the niche.

In the *Entombment* the artist expresses himself in even more sonorous and monumental terms. Opening behind the group of figures, in the flaked mass of the rock, is the dark mouth of the tomb, geometrically cut and decorated with reliefs below. The white shroud makes thin sculptural pleats on the body of Christ and unfolds on the grass, abruptly creating a suggestion of depth in the otherwise horizontal development of the composition.

FRA ANGELICO
Entombment (1440–42)
Tempera on panel; 14 1/2″ × 18″.
It came to the Alte Pinakothek in
1832 from the collection of
Ludwig I of Bavaria.

ANTONELLO DA MESSINA. *Virgin of the Annunciation.* *p. 120*
Writing in 1660, Boschini reported that a picture in the house of Ottavio
Tassis of a "Madonna with a book in front" had no match for fineness
among all such studies in the world; this panel has been identified with the
painting he was describing. Like other single figures by Antonello — Ma-
donnas, Christs, portraits — it has been studied and constructed essentially
in volumetric terms. Compact in its uniform blue impasto, the mantle encloses the head and shoulders. The fold above the forehead, the line of the 119

FRA FILIPPO LIPPI
Florence circa 1406 — Spoleto 1469
Active mainly in Tuscany, except for a so-
journ in Padua (1434). Around 1452 he
executed the frescoes in the choir of the
Cathedral of Prato; in 1467–69, those in
the Cathedral of Spoleto.
Annunciation (circa 1443–45)
Tempera on panel; 6'8" × 6'1 1/4". From
an altar in the Convento delle Murate in
Florence. It came to the Alte Pinakothek
from the collection of the royal house of
Bavaria.

ANTONELLO DA MESSINA
Messina circa 1430 — Messina 1479
Pupil of Colantonio in Naples, he worked
mainly in Sicily and later (1475–76) in
Venice; but was also in Rome, where he
probably knew Piero della Francesca, and
in Milan, etc.
Virgin of the Annunciation
Oil on panel; 17" × 12 1/2". Perhaps half
of a diptych with another panel, now lost,
representing the *Angel of the Annunciation.*
The surface of the painting has no glazes
and shows some damage. From a private
collection (1897).

nose and the inner edges of the mantle converge by different paths toward
the crossed hands, and from here — notice the slight bending at the wrist —
moves on to the oblique fold of the missal. The setting is reduced to the
minimum. A balustrade seen obliquely, covered with a strip of damask,
holds the missal and another little volume tied with a strap; the latter, bright
red on the yellow marble, helps establish the thickness of the space on which
it rests. The face is turned to the left following the glance toward an image
that is not visible to us and perhaps is only something imagined by the young
girl. The hands are asymmetrically arranged, and the long, extended fingers
elude the cadence of the mantle.

FRA FILIPPO LIPPI. *Annunciation.*

Because of some references to Fra Angelico's art, this painting was once
held to be a youthful work of Lippi's; it was subsequently recognized as belonging to a more advanced moment in the artist's career. This was the period around or after 1440, when — after his phases of high enthusiasm for
Masaccio, Jacopo della Quercia and Donatello — he returned to Fra Angelico's influence. It should be stated, however, that a certain thinning of the

121

forms and the slightly more controlled, classicizing framework, do not substantially alter Lippi's pictorial language. The artist was disposed to absorb different experiences and to combine elements from various sources. Notice the ground plane divided by steps and parapets. The perspective is not completely consistent, and contrasting architectural elements are brought together: pilasters and columns, arches and beams. Then there are the many details lovingly portrayed, such as the glass vase, the complicated lectern, the dove and the lilies. Finally, there are the apparitions that are not strictly in accordance with iconographic tradition: God the Father (top left), with several angels, on clouds flaked like rocks; and the full-figured angel looking in from the left, as if by chance. In that figure it is possible that Lippi wanted to show the development of the action by portraying Gabriel in two successive positions, on arrival and then kneeling before the Madonna.

122

SANDRO BOTTICELLI
Florence 1445 — Florence 1510
Pupil of Fra Filippo Lippi, he worked mainly in Florence. In 1481 and 1482 he was in Rome for his part in the decoration of the Sistine Chapel.
Pietà (circa 1495–1500)
Tempera on panel; 3'7 1/4" × 6'9 1/2". From the church of S. Paolino in Florence. A pupil probably assisted in the final stages of the painting. From the collection of Ludwig I of Bavaria.

SANDRO BOTTICELLI. *Pietà.*

In his late activity, Botticelli sometimes gave up his architectural frameworks to concentrate mainly on the figures, which he constructed according to his own canons of proportion rather than by objective standards of reproducing reality. Here the group is framed only by the heavy backdrop of stone, the sarcophagus is half hidden in the background and the artist's interest is concentrated on the figures. These are St. Peter, St. Paul and St. Jerome, who look on from positions somewhat to the rear; Mary Magdalene, at the feet of Christ; and John the Evangelist and the two Holy Women, who lean forward or kneel to support the half-fainting Madonna and Christ. The last figure has gone limp in a long curve that is the major motive of the composition. The dark and acid red, green, orange and yellow tonalities and the flushed or livid flesh colors accentuate the intensity of the drama, which the artist seems to invite us to consider as the theme of human impotence in the face of evil. Michelangelo certainly knew this painting and appreciated the lyrical suffering shown in Christ's smooth, arched body, from whose skin the light draws the most refined textual effects.

PIERO DI COSIMO. *The Myth of Prometheus.*

The front of a *cassone,* or a decorative wall panel, this work and its pendant in Strasbourg represent the Prometheus myth according to a late version in which the hero is responsible not only for the theft of fire but also for the creation of man. The latter event is in fact shown at the left of the Alte Pinakothek's panel; there Prometheus is seen shaping man with the help of his brother, Epimetheus. In the center the image is brought to life by divine fire,

PIERO DI COSIMO
Florence circa 1462 — Florence 1521
A pupil of Cosimo Rosselli, he trained himself by studying Leonardo and Filippino Lippi. Throughout his career, he worked in Florence, executing altarpieces and numerous smaller works.
The Myth of Prometheus (circa 1515) Oil on panel; 26 3/4″ × 46 3/4″. It came to the Alte Pinakothek in 1817 from the Kauffmann collection in Berlin. Its companion panel has been in the Museum of Strasbourg since 1896.

123

while on the right Prometheus receives Minerva and then follows her. In the Strasbourg panel the account concludes with the punishment of the hero, whose liver is eaten by an eagle, at Jupiter's command. The theme has allowed the artist to produce refined subtleties in color and a fluid narrative development, probably related to 16th-century theatrical performances.

LEONARDO DA VINCI. *Madonna and Child.*

The attribution of this painting has been long debated, but today it seems to be definitively accepted as a work of the young Leonardo — although the damages suffered by the painting would suggest caution. There is no contemporary of Leonardo's to whom so free and mobile a composition might be assigned. It betrays a decided intolerance of any form of established order, especially for the "measure" peculiar to Florentine tradition, which had already been breached in some respects by Andrea del Verrocchio, Leonardo's master. Placed in the shadow of a large room, the seated Madonna offers a carnation to the child who seems to be rising from the wrinkled cushion. Without making use of perspective lines, the artist succeeds in separating the figures from the background wall, as well as the wall from the landscape. A raking light runs along the folds of the dress curling in every direction; it strikes the hair and the undulating veil raised on the head; and it touches the rising rotundities of the child. Distracting our attention from the real subject, the light lingers in the tangle of pleats opening out of the yellow lining of the mantle, which was intentionally so arranged on the model by the artist. Finally, it strikes the glass vase containing flowers, which has no material consistency and exists only through the flickering light reflections. Beyond the windows there is the well-known landscape typical of Leonardo, from which any sign of human presence has been removed. Its extent is indeterminate, and the mobility and remoteness of its dramatic, eroded forms are accentuated by the bluish haze that hangs over them.

RAPHAEL. *The Canigiani Holy Family.*   *p. 126*

Executed around 1507, this is a mature and knowledgeable work of the precocious artist. Already Raphael's Florentine experience had rounded out his Umbrian education in the art of Piero della Francesca and Perugino; moreover he had assimilated all that two such formidable innovators as Leonardo and Michelangelo could offer him at that period. Evident here is the influence of Leonardo's compositions, and at the same time there is a knowledge of the spiral motion and the dynamic plastic cohesion pursued by Michelangelo. The squatting figures of St. Elizabeth and the Madonna define a space in the foreground that is occupied by the two children, and with a rotary movement — St. Elizabeth is closer to the spectator, while the Madonna's head is inclined toward the interior of the picture — the composition is drawn in the direction of Joseph. He bends his knee slightly as he leans over the group, supporting himself firmly on a long staff, and his halo, with its closed circular form concludes the interconnected development of the forms. Peculiar to Raphael is the orderly, balanced structure of the group, which is modeled in resplendent impastoes of color that emphasize the lucid consistency of the drapery and the figures. Appropriately, the group is placed in an everyday countryside, with its succession of grassy knolls and its familiar buildings.

LEONARDO DA VINCI
Vinci 1452 — Amboise 1519
Painter, sculptor and architect, he also devoted himself to speculative thought and scientific research. Active mainly in Florence (1470–82; 1500–1506) and Milan. In 1517 he went to France as a guest of Francis I.
Madonna and Child (circa 1478)
Oil on panel; 24 1/2″ × 18 1/2″. It entered the Alte Pinakothek in 1889, from the Haug collection in Günzburg. The surface is seamed with *craquelures* and numerous passages are partially repainted. The Louvre has a Flemish copy of this work.

RAPHAEL
Urbino 1483 — Rome 1520
Fresco and easel painter, and architect as
well. Active mainly in Umbria; in Florence,
where he went for the first time early in
the 1500's; and in Rome, where his presence is documented from 1509.
The Canigiani Holy Family (circa 1507)
Oil on panel; 51 1/2″ × 42″.
On the hem of the Madonna's scarf is the inscription: "RAPHAEL. URBINAS." Painted
for Domenico Canigiani, in the house of
whose heirs Vasari saw it. It entered the
Medici collection, and when Anna Maria
Luisa, daughter of Cosimo III married the
Elector Palatine Johann Wilhelm she
brought it with her to Düsseldorf. In 1801
it was moved to Munich.

RAPHAEL. *Tempi Madonna.*

This work belongs to the final moment of Raphael's activity in Florence.
Compared to other paintings, such as the splendid but highly intellectual
Madonna del Granduca or the complex *Ansidei Madonna* in the National
Gallery, London, which are dated between 1504 and 1506, the *Tempi Madonna* is free of any conscious effort to show his worth with respect to his
more illustrious contemporaries. In the limpid evening air, the Madonna
turns to one side as she lightly presses the child to herself, while her mantle
swells around her, creating a monumental effect. Only two tonalities — the
pink sapped by the light and the blue that is tenuous in sky and landscape
but dense in the mantle — enhance the compact texture of the rosy skin and
the fine blond hair. Every conflict is calmed, and the idea of maternity
shared both in human and in divine nature is set forth in unalterable purity.

RAPHAEL
Tempi Madonna
(circa 1507–8)
Oil on panel; 30 1/4″ × 21 3/4″.
Executed for the Tempi family, in
whose house it was seen by Cinelli.
Acquired in 1829 by Ludwig I of Bavaria.

RAPHAEL
Madonna della Tenda (circa 1514)
Oil on panel; 26″ × 20 1/4″.
Formerly in the Escorial, then in
England in the 19th century, where it
was acquired by Ludwig I of Bavaria.

RAPHAEL. *Madonna della Tenda.*

Contemporary with or a little later than the main frescoes in the Vatican
Stanze, this work belongs to the group of paintings and drawings that accompanied the preparation of the famous *Madonna della Seggiola*. The interrelationship of the figures here is more complex than in Raphael's youthful solutions. Going beyond proportional and harmonious systems, the artist
ruthlessly cuts elements of the composition at the edges of the panel, and en-
twines the limbs of the figures, with some relaxed and others in dynamic tension. Note the torso of the Madonna, which goes back with respect to her
head; and the abrupt turn of the child, sustained by the diagonal edge of the
curtain, which is balanced by St. John's appearance. Fuller form in greater
chiaroscuro also shows the change in the artist's direction. At this period,
after the death of Bramante and the departure of Michelangelo, Raphael
was on his way to becoming the chief figure in the Roman art world.

LORENZO LOTTO. *Mystic Marriage of St. Catherine.*

This panel shows the formal perfection and the complex cultural influences present in Lotto's early work. In this composition one is struck by the rigorously pyramidal composition, which the artist had already tried in the *Assumption* at Asolo, and which perhaps reflects a model dear to Leonardo. The closed forms of the figures that make up the pyramid's facetings in space are well suited to the pyramidal framework. Their strict construction, deriving from Antonello da Messina, is softened by the sensitivity of the light, especially in the child leaning anxiously toward St. Catherine. Lotto miraculously endows that saint with a spirituality that does not alter her almost peasant candor. This sensitivity in the light effects gives Lotto the idea of having the pensive figure of Joseph, as severe as a Dürer, appear on the right, out of the shadow.

LORENZO LOTTO
Venice circa 1480 — Loreto 1556
*Mystic Marriage of
St. Catherine* (1506–7)
Panel; 28″ × 35 3/4″.
It is not known how or when the painting reached the Archiepiscopal Castle of Würzburg, from which it came to the Alte Pinakothek. Among the old literary sources, only Ridolfi speaks of a *Marriage of St. Catherine,* which was seen in Treviso in the house of the Ridolfi family; some scholars identify it with this one. In the Boston Museum of Fine Arts there is a copy with variations. A drawing for the Madonna is in the Gabinetto Nazionale delle Stampe in Rome.

TITIAN
Pieve di Cadore 1488–90 — Venice 1576
Portrait of a Man (1512–13)
Panel; 27 1/4″ × 20 3/4″.
From the Electoral Gallery of Munich,
which acquired it in 1748. Identified by some
scholars with the work cited by Vasari and
Ridolfi as in the Fugger household and from
the hand of Giorgione. Also attributed to
Giorgione in a print by W. Hollar, in 1650.

JACOPO DE' BARBARI
Venice (?) circa 1450 — circa 1516
Still Life (1504)
Lime panel; 20 1/4″ × 16 3/4″.
Brought from Neuburg on the Danube in
1804. The scrap of paper represented in the
lower right bears the inscription "Jac. de
Barbarj p. 1504" and the caduceus, which
is the symbol used by the artist in his nu-
merous prints.

JACOPO DE' BARBARI. *Still Life.*

A modest hunting trophy is shown in this splendid little panel. The painting
looks as if it had been done with an illuminator's brush — indeed, "painter
and illuminator" was the title under which the Emperor Maximilian took
Jacopo de' Barbari into his service in 1500. A partridge, revealing the delicate nuances of its tiny feathers, hangs on the wall with two steel gauntlets
and an arrow. Although there is a minute attention to every detail, the happy
synthesis of the objects seen against the light ground is not lost, and the small
work becomes emblematic for this mysterious artist, as a link between the
cultural trends of Italy and the north. The painting was done at the end of
one of Jacopo's numerous stays in Germany (1502–4). His Venetian education, in the circle of Alvise Vivarini, must have given him the aura of a
modern Italian painter among the Germans, who were avid for Renaissance
novelty.

TITIAN. *Portrait of a Man.*

There has been a great deal of controversy over the attribution of this work,
described as the portrait of "a German of the House of Fugger wearing a fox
fur, seen from the side as he turns." Both Giorgione and Palma il Vecchio

131

have been cited as the author, whereas modern critics think that the work is by Titian. The idea of a figure seen from the back is Giorgionesque — as in the *Portrait of Gerolamo Marcello* cited by Michiel — but here it is carried out in a very different manner. The subject turns towards us with an almost defiant look, pressing his lips together and clutching a glove in his right hand. The aggressive face is built up without any mysterious half-shadows, in broad lighted planes framed by the thick hair. A wonderful mastery and a feeling for materials allow the painter to render perfectly the soft, red fox-fur jacket from which the padded magenta sleeve emerges. All these elements lead us back to Titian. For the dating, probably one should not go too far from the frescoes in the Scuola del Santo (1510–11) at Padua. Even the hint of a story, suggested by the manner of presenting the figure, is connected with that moment of Titian's personal affirmation, in contrast with the subtle problems besetting Giorgione's contemporary creations.

TITIAN. *Charles V Seated.*

In January, 1548, Titian was called to Augsburg by Charles V, who had convoked the Diet there after the victory of Mühlberg over the Protestant League. He thus became the official portrait painter of the Emperor and one of the most important members of the court. The painter had brought with him his son Orazio, his relative, Cesare Vecellio and his pupil, Lambert Sustris. His busy studio also took in local artists, like Christoph Amberger, who subsequently restored *Charles V on Horseback* (Prado) which Titian executed in the spring of 1548. The equestrian portrait precedes this depiction of the Emperor seated in a loggia opening on a landscape. Whereas the first portrait has been described as "the exaltation of a personage seen in the light of a myth," here Titian is concerned with fidelity to the image and perfection of detail — as if in rivalry with the northern portraiture to which his patrons were accustomed. Otherwise there is no explanation for the precision with which the face stands out from the black of the hat, or with which the black shapes of the legs stand out against the red floor. But in the color, the Venetian in Titian comes to the fore, with an orchestration of wonderful, compact blacks in the clothes, which are accentuated by the tones of the somewhat muted reds of the velvet on the armchair. The unusual landscape, with its light, liquid, almost immaterial tones, presents a problem. It is probable that Lambert Sustris, Titian's pupil, finished the work or was responsible for a later restoration.

TITIAN. *Holy Family and Donor.*   *p. 134*

In affinity of subject and form, the composition belongs to a small group of works including the *Holy Family and Donor* in Edinburgh and the *Holy Family and Shepherd* in the National Gallery, London. These contemporary works, dating from 1513 to 1514, are splendid in color and are extraordinarily integrated in form, as if the placing of the groups in the open were intended to bring out their structural values. However, in critical appraisals up to the present day, they have often been disclaimed as Titian's and ascribed to copyists or pupils like Bordone. They are elegant in arrangement, display a richness of shining silks and give glimpses of nature that make a setting which does not blend with the figures, as in the late works of Giorgione. Giorgione's inspiration was indeed carried to its ultimate conse-

132

TITIAN
Charles V Seated (1548)
Canvas; 6'8 3/4" × 3'8 3/4"
(or 3'11 1/2" with the addition).
Signed: "Titianus. F. MDXLVIII."
From the Electoral Gallery of Munich;
it was painted in Augsburg probably for
the Duke of Bavaria, during Titian's
first visit, in 1548.

quences by Titian, but here the inspiration is more archaic. Titian's elaboration is mainly concerned with the complex dynamics of the figures, their harmonious interrelationship and their placing in an atmosphere of light and quiet that is almost idyllic.

TITIAN. *Profane Love (Vanity)*.
Variously titled, this picture has interested many scholars because of the problems in iconology that it poses. Debate has been stimulated especially by the detail of the mirror and what it reflects: trinkets and an old woman spinning. X-ray examination has shown that in the first sketch the woman was holding her hair in her hand, as in the *Girl Combing Her Hair* in the Louvre, and that the images in the mirror were added later. Recalling a similar figure by Lambert Sustris, Titian's assistant, one critic proposes that these additions be attributed to him, at the time when he and his master were staying in Augsburg. The painting belongs to a group of half-length female figures built on the same scheme, whose highest and most famous example is the *Flora* (1516) in the Uffizi. Here the model is seen almost frontally, with her head tilted slightly toward the left; her rosy bust is revealed by the low blouse, like a flower emerging from its calyx.

TITIAN. *Crowning with Thorns*.
This large *Crowning with Thorns* repeats almost exactly the composition in the Louvre, which Titian executed some thirty years earlier for the church of

Left:
TITIAN
Holy Family and Donor (1513–14)
Canvas; 29 1/2″ × 36 1/4″.
From the gallery of the Elector Johann Wilhelm in Düsseldorf, but belonged to the great gallery of pictures assembled from Italian collections by the Archduke Leopold Wilhelm in the mid-17th century. There is a late and not particularly faithful copy in the Bucharest Museum.

Above:
TITIAN
Profane Love (Vanity) (1514–15)
Canvas; 38 1/4″ × 31 3/4″.
From the Electoral Gallery in Munich; according to tradition it was formerly in Rudolph II's gallery in Prague. Morelli assigned it to Titian (1880); Hetzer and Tietze suspected that it might be a copy, but today scholars agree that it is Titian's work. The X-ray examination reported by Verheyan in 1966 revealed corrections and additions.

TITIAN
Crowning with Thorns (circa 1570)
Canvas; 9′2 1/4″ × 5′11 3/4″.
From the gallery of the Elector of Bavaria. Von Hadlen identified it as the canvas belonging to Jacopo Tintoretto, which was sold by his son, Domenico, to "a northerner and a connoisseur," as Boschini writes.

Santa Maria delle Grazie in Milan. A comparison between the two is useful
in defining Titian's supreme pictorial language in this image. The painting
in the Louvre represents the moment in which elements of Mannerist influence push the master to an almost excessive degree of tension in psychology
and form. Christ's pain is represented through the medium of a knowledge
136 of the *Laocoön,* and the brutality of his tormentors explodes in a tangle of

TINTORETTO
Venice 1518 — Venice 1594
Venus, Vulcan and Mars
Canvas; 4'4 3/4" × 6'5 3/4".
The work was acquired in 1925 from the
Kaulbach collection, and before that its per-
egrinations in France and England (Coll.
Munro) can be traced. It is not known for
whom it was executed.

powerful limbs revolving in space. But here, against the gloom of the background lighted by smoky torches, the figures of the victim and his persecutors loom up mysteriously and are compounded of a material mixing light and ashes, light and mud. There is a fascination like that of Rembrandt, yet even more dramatic since the fine-grained vibrancy that enriches the Dutch master's canvases is lacking. The exhausted Christ submits to the cruel blows. Tired executioners are urged on by a young official. A boy holds more sticks that may be required to continue the torture. Even the sky, with its mass of funereal clouds, appears to participate in the scene. Boschini, writing in 1674, reported that "Palma told me, in truth, that in the finishing [Titian] painted more with his fingers than with his brushes." Certain glowing touches and quivers of light could not have been put on this canvas in any other way by the great old man.

TINTORETTO. *Venus, Vulcan and Mars.*
Tintoretto's repertory of secular subjects is not very large, but when he devoted himself to one of these themes, as in dealing with this classical myth, he brought to it all of his powers. Here we have Venus trying to cover herself with a sheet, Vulcan pulling away the covering and Mars ill-concealed under the table, while Cupid — the malicious instigator of the situation — pretends to be asleep by the window. The event takes place in a room in a fine Venetian palace, with prismatic windows, a Murano glass vase on the windowsill and a mirror on the wall reflecting the scene. What is striking is the strong diffused light and the highly balanced orchestration of color that reaches to Venus' mass of fine blond hair, the variegated sash around Vulcan's loins and the delicate skin of Cupid. All these details date the picture to shortly after 1550. This was the period during which Tintoretto's color reflected Veronese's clear palette, and a study of Mannerist work had led him to give his figures greater elegance and flexibility. The measuring of space by the oblique disposition of limbs is a highly personal development, but the perspective recession of the floor patterns and the coordination of the light sources still give a balanced feeling. It is perhaps the only painting by Tintoretto for which a complete drawing exists.

TINTORETTO. *Christ in the House of Martha and Mary.*   p. 138
This work is certainly not made to strike the imagination, nor to excite strong reactions. It is a rather unusual Tintoretto, in the controlled development of the narrative aspects and in the almost refined finish of the descriptive detail. The psychological ties connecting the three principal figures have their compositional metaphor in the closed structure in which the group is inscribed. Rich but not gaudy, the color seems almost excessively controlled, as does the light that reveals every facet of reality, including Mary's trinkets, the copper pots hung in the corner of the kitchen and the figure of the maid by the hearth, showing the reflections of the flames. On further study, however, it is precisely this intimacy that gives the painting its fascination. It is likely that such a work would have come before the period in which Tintoretto's imaginative violence was unleashed on the great enterprise of the upper hall of S. Rocco (1576–88). But disquieting details are not lacking: with his hands silhouetted against the light tablecloth, Christ seems less to be

TINTORETTO
Christ in the House of
Martha and Mary (1570–75)
Canvas; 6'5 3/4" × 51 1/2".
From the Dominican church in Augsburg.
It bears the inscription:
"Jacobus Tintoretus F."

persuading the woman seated — not humbly — at his feet, than attracting her by hypnotic force.

JACOPO BASSANO. *Altarpiece.*

The Madonna and Child appear to us between St. James the Greater and St. John the Baptist. From the height of her throne she seems to follow the dialogue between the two saints, who are wasted creatures with somewhat hallucinated countenances and sensitive hands. An uninterrupted vibration

JACOPO BASSANO
Bassano 1517–18 — Bassano 1592
Altarpiece (1545–50)
Canvas; 6'3 1/4" × 4'4 1/4".
Painted for the Church at Tomo (Feltre).
According to old sources (Verci) it was purloined by the painter, G. B. Volpato, a plagiarist of Bassano. It went to the Bassano Monte di Pietà and was sold at auction in 1695. From the Electoral Gallery of Düsseldorf.

agitates the folds of their garments, the Madonna's mantle and the white veils around her noble head. It is all a play of alternating light and dark areas. Although the color is parched and has deteriorated, the work has a refined elegance and the orchestration of the composition obeys interior laws rather than pursuing naturalistic likeness. These considerations suggest placing the work, which is not chronologically documented, at the heart of Jacopo Bassano's Mannerist period, or between 1545 and 1550. Those are the years in which the innovations brought to Venice by Roman and Tuscan painters in the decade from 1530 to 1540 transformed the climate of Venetian painting. At that time, Bassano, who had started as a pupil of Bonifazio de' Pitati and later acquired the strict form of Pordenone, reached a new conception of elegance in form through the study of Parmigianino's prints. But Venetian art of this period is always a complex reflection of many currents. In this altarpiece, besides the linear, almost wavy structure of Parmigianino, perhaps it is also possible to make out a particular recollection of the first generation of Mannerism. The St. John the Baptist, with his wild head and his hooked hand, reminds us of certain intense features in Rosso Fiorentino and in Pontormo.

GIOVANNI BATTISTA TIEPOLO. *Adoration of the Magi.*

Giovanni Battista Tiepolo arrived at Würzburg on December 12, 1750, with his sons Domenico and Lorenzo, at the command of Prince Bishop Carl Philip von Greifenklau, who wished to have a hall in his Residence frescoed. The stay was longer than anticipated, as the patron was full of admiration for the first paintings in the Kaisersaal, and ordered the decoration of the immense ceiling over the stairs. But fresco work could not be carried out during the season of bad weather; and the Venetian master — besides preparing an infinite number of drawings and sketches for the frescoes — devoted himself, with his usual conscientiousness, to easel painting for churches and private clients. Perhaps the most important of these commissions was the great *Adoration of the Magi* in the Alte Pinakothek. Through Tiepolo's taste for spectacle, the *Adoration* becomes a theme exalting divinity over the earthly powers. The execution of the Würzburg frescoes had given Tiepolo's brush a sureness and a bold gaiety, and the extraordinarily luminous color here creates solid forms that are structured from within and expand into the space. Even though he may slide into the hyperbole with the gorgeous appearance of the Moorish king, the composition is perfectly controlled. For the first time in his repertory, he introduced the novelty of the northern peasant types, borrowed from Rubens and Jordaens, whose work Tiepolo had seen in German princely collections. The color is held to an exceptionally high-keyed range of light tones. In the sumptuous silk mantle of the kneeling king, the inclusion of a more or less warm tone of cream is a virtuoso feat. The coordinating element is always the strong light, which firmly models the structures, as may be seen in the regal face of the Madonna. It is allied to the quivering dark line used for underlining and to the luminous flicks on drapery, greenery and still life.

FRANCESCO GUARDI. *Concert.* *p. 142*

It is really curious that fate should have reserved to a painter as imaginative, gifted and lyrical as Guardi the task of executing documentary paintings of events like Pius VI's official visit to Venice, the marriage of the Prince de

GIOVANNI BATTISTA TIEPOLO
Venice 1696 — Madrid 1770
Adoration of the Magi (1753)
Canvas; 13'11 1/4" × 6'10 3/4".
The altarpiece was ordered for the Benedictine church in Schwarzach, and was delivered in 1753. In 1804 it entered the Hofgartengalerie in Munich. Inscribed: "GIO. B. TIEPOLO F. A. 1753."

Polignac or the ascent of Count Zambeccari's hot-air balloon. Of a series celebrating the visit to Venice in 1782 of the Grand Duke Paul Petrovitch and the Grand Duchess Maria Feodorovna, only three have survived, and this is the finest. The scene shows an elegant crowd gathered in the Sala dei Filarmonici, which is in one of the buildings on St. Mark's Square. We may imagine the painter in a corner of the hall, feverishly making sketches in order to reconstruct the spectacle in his studio. In the painting here he has recreated with extraordinary vivacity the aesthetic enjoyment provided by the sumptuousness of the silks, the glittering of the Murano chandeliers and the charm of the music, which was performed by the famous girl students of the Istituto della Pietà. We see them on the left, in the wooden loge with its exquisitely rococo curves. However, there is something more in this recreation: not the subtle irony of a Longhi, nor the sarcastic allusions of a Domenico Tiepolo, but rather the sorrowful sensation that this attractive world and these creatures as slight as butterflies are so very fragile. Before the view of his decaying and crumbling city, as well as before the spectacle of this brilliant and insecure society, Guardi becomes the poet of a changing world and expresses the most belated and exquisite aspects of Venetian life.

142

FRANCESCO GUARDI
Venice 1712 — Venice 1793
Concert (1782)
Canvas; 26 3/4″ × 35 1/2″.
Acquired at a sale in England in 1909. Executed with five other paintings in 1782, perhaps on a government commission, to commemorate the visit to Venice of the "Counts of the North," the Russian Grand Duke Paul Petrovitch and the Grand Duchess Maria Feodorovna.

SPAIN

EL GRECO (DOMENICO THEOTOKOPOULOS). *Disrobing of Christ.*

The celebrated representation of the *Disrobing* — a new and unique iconographic subject — was commissioned by the canons of the Cathedral of Toledo shortly after El Greco's arrival in the Spanish city, in July, 1577. He completed the work in 1579. Numerous copies exist, but this one is certainly by the artist's hand and may be dated around 1583–84. Smaller than the original version by half, it is more elongated in proportion and more crowded in the rotary movement of the figures. Although the general color scheme is less livid than the original, the picture preserves intact all of the prototype's bold and novel solutions.

The grandiose mass of the red-clad Christ, the only element shown frontally in the whole crowded composition, stands motionless and distracted in the center. In the Toledo version this is the real center; here, in this second version, it is only the ideal center. The displacement of Christ to the side frees the entire work of a certain symmetrical constriction and permits the revolving motion that is its most peculiar feature. Crowded to a convulsive degree, the painting shows another typical characteristic of the blazing creations of the artist: total indifference to any realistic arrangement or gradation of the successive planes in the picture. The Three Marys, in the left foreground, stand on imaginary ground that is much lower than the bottom of the composition. The ground shown under the feet of Christ, the man in armor and the two executioners is almost vertical it is so unrealistically inclined. Above, all the hallucinatory creatures, with their almost caricatured heads, explode on the surface in a space so cramped and compressed that it is impossible to imagine that they are standing in any actual space.

DIEGO VELÁZQUEZ DE SILVA. *Portrait of a Young Man. p. 146*
Wrongly considered a self-portrait, or sometimes taken to be a portrait of the Infante Don Fernando because of the subject's somewhat Bourbon features, this work has been dated by art critics between 1626 and 1631, but the earlier date is more likely because of the painting's closeness to Velázquez' youthful style. The romantic suggestion as well as the strength of the face are emphasized by the neutral ground on which the unrelieved mass of the bust in its somber, unadorned garb, has been delineated. The passage with the hand indicated only in rapid black strokes is a typical example of the artist's much discussed "unfinished" effects. In his works this is sometimes seen where a picture has in fact not been completed, probably for circumstantial reasons, but this is rare. Otherwise, as in the present case, and also in religious and mythological subjects, some part of a picture that in other respects has been completed will be left in the state of a summary sketch. The striking contrast here, between the expressive intensity of the nobly bemused face and the deliberate austerity of the figure and ground, leads us to believe that the hand is intentionally unfinished, so as to eliminate a possibly disturbing element. At the same time it is perhaps a way of making us aware of the process used by the artist to create his images on the canvas.

144

FRANCISCO DE ZURBARÁN. *St. Francis.*

Living in the Baroque Age, in a country that had its greatest flowering in the arts during that period, Zurbarán nevertheless preserved the robust medieval tradition in his sober, rigidly composed and clearly drawn personages. The subjects, however, have a new appearance under Zurbarán's stronger light. An obstinately religious painter in theme, he gives his mystic and ecstatic subjects a natural air, respecting the ordinary appearance of people and things. In the silent, stable, solemn universe that he creates, Zurbarán always avoids any suggestion of drama or passion. The sobriety of technique, the concentration of action and the control in composition — which are all constant in the artist's work — are especially evident in this *St. Francis,* painted in Madrid during the final years of Zurbarán's tormented existence. Six similar versions are known (without counting about thirty in different poses), showing his habit of reflecting on and returning often to the same subject. It should be added, however, that this practice also allowed his workshop to produce numerous versions, though these are apt to be poor and feeble.

146

Left:
DIEGO VELÁZQUEZ DE SILVA
Seville 1599 — Madrid 1660
Portrait of a Young Man (1626–31)
Canvas; 35 1/4" × 27 1/4".
Acquired in Madrid by the Ambassador Wiser for the Elector Johann Wilhelm (1694), it was moved in 1805 from the Düsseldorf Gallery to Munich. The identity of the subject is unknown.

Above:
FRANCISCO DE ZURBARÁN
Fuente de Cantos (Badajoz) 1598 — living in Madrid in 1664
St. Francis
Canvas; 25 1/2" × 20 3/4".
Formerly in the Mannheim Gallery, it was moved to Munich in 1836.
Six versions are known, some of them workshop pieces.

BARTOLOMÉ ESTEBAN MURILLO
Seville 1618 — Seville 1682
*St. Thomas of Villanueva
Distributing Alms*
Canvas; 7'2 1/2" × 4'10 3/4".
Acquired in Paris in 1815 by
General Sebastiani.

BARTOLOMÉ ESTEBAN MURILLO. *St. Thomas of Villanueva
Distributing Alms.*

This work is sometimes confused with another, fuller and more complex scene from the life of the alms-giving saint, which Murillo painted for the chapel of the Augustinian Convent in Seville in 1768 (Northbrook collection, London). It was certainly executed during the artist's last years and shows him in a less typical aspect, though abiding by his formal features. The principal figures of the narrative are arranged in the foreground on a triangular plan, both on the surface and in depth, and are set apart by the somber architectural ground and the oblique and slightly raised marble step. Behind them, on the left, there is an unexpected and unusual glimpse of a town square with Renaissance buildings and a number of small, animated figures. The high, diagonal viewpoint makes this vivid picture of cheerful daily life recede even more from the solemn and pious main episode, and gives it the value of a deliberate contrast.

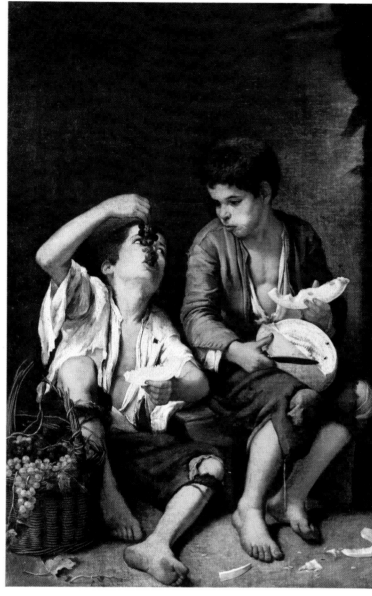

BARTOLOMÉ ESTEBAN MURILLO. *Girls Selling Fruit* and *Boys Eating Fruit.*

These also are works of Murillo's maturity — executed presumably around 1670 — as is shown by the insistence on strong chiaroscuro; the assurance, the almost excessive bravura in the still-life passages; the soft, sweet faces; the iridescent materials and the nuances of the grounds. There is, in sum, an absolute mastery of a technique that has reached almost automatic perfection. Genre pictures like these sweetened images of working-class children, which the artist painted throughout his career, are often interpreted as the realistic, social and anti-conformist work of the painter, who was otherwise concerned with religious, sentimental and refined works. But an artfully torn shirt and a muddy bare foot are not enough to make protest manifestations out of these pleasingly anecdotal little scenes. They are merely

Left:
BARTOLOMÉ ESTEBAN MURILLO
Girls Selling Fruit (1670?)
Canvas; 56 1/4″ × 42″ (original size; the two canvases have had strips about two centimeters wide added at the sides). From Mannheim. It was inherited by Counselor Franz Jos von Dufresne with its pendant, *The Toilette,* which is also in the Alte Pinakothek.

Above:
BARTOLOMÉ ESTEBAN MURILLO
Boys Eating Fruit (1670?)
Canvas; 56 1/4″ × 41 1/4″.
From the Mannheim Gallery in 1788.

pretexts for figures and compositions that have the same qualities as the artist's more official, religious production.

FRANCISCO DE GOYA Y LUCIENTES. *Portrait of Don José Queralto.*

Even under French domination, Goya went on with his work as court painter, portraying the personalities around the ephemeral King Joseph. One of these, Joseph Quérault (as he was known in French), a general and a doctor, is shown here in his splendid uniform decorated with gleaming red and gold braid. It is a noble portrait even though the composition is traditional and hackneyed, and the face, though individual, conveys a fatigue, a lack of interest unusual in the artist's work. A highly skilled performance,

FRANCISCO DE GOYA Y LUCIENTES
Fuendetodos 1746 — Bordeaux 1828
Portrait of Don José Queralto (1802?)
Canvas; 40 1/4″ × 30″.
Signed on the note in the subject's hand:
"Don Josef Queralto por Goya 1809."
Formerly in the Bohler collection
in Munich, it was acquired by the
Alte Pinakothek in 1925.

149

the work was part of official routine during the sorrowful years of the occupation. At the same time, in his engravings called *The Disasters of War*, Goya was recording with desperate intensity the struggles, the suffering, the illusions and defeats of a people — and a man — who believed and hoped that Liberty and Truth were changing the course of history.

FRANCISCO DE GOYA Y LUCIENTES. *Still Life.*

To the tired and disillusioned artist, it must have been a comfort and a refuge to work on the still lifes he painted during the years of the occupation (twelve are listed in the studio inventory of 1812) and subsequently during his exile in France. There he arrived after the harsh reaction of 1823, looking, his friends said, "old, deaf and feeble . . . yet happy and eager to see the world." It was a world of simple things, such as the market at Bordeaux, teeming with people and things, where he looked for subjects, which he took home and painted "all in one breath." Certainly it must have been the case for this raw, powerful picture, in which the masterful arrangement and the sumptuous color are accompanied by the infinite sadness of the poor, slaughtered creature, another victim of the horrors that men perpetrate.

150

FRANCISCO DE GOYA Y LUCIENTES
Still Life
Canvas; 17 1/2″ × 24 1/2″.
Signed lower left: "Goya." From the
Astruc collection, it was bought on
the Paris art market in 1909.

FRANCE

MASTER OF MOULINS. *Portrait of Charles II of Bourbon.*

One of the most fascinating and debated personalities of the French Early Renaissance is the so-called Master of Moulins, who takes his name from the anonymous masterpiece in the cathedral of Moulins. The cathedral's triptych is generally dated around 1488 from the age shown in the portrait there — the same subject as in this work by the same hand — of Cardinal Charles of Bourbon, who had been Archbishop of Lyons since 1485. The figure, shown half-length in three-quarter view, is arranged like a portrait by van Eyck, with that realism derived from the Gothic which is nevertheless anti-romantic, strictly rational and modern. In addition the figure has an intensely pietistic vein that relates it to Hugo van der Goes' types.

ANTOINE CARON. *Portrait of a Lady.*

This work, although controlled in the stylized apathy of the subject, expresses a somewhat disconcerting inner life. A subtle perturbation tinges

MASTER OF MOULINS
Active between 1475 and 1500
Portrait of Charles II of Bourbon
Tempera on panel; 13 1/2″ × 9 3/4″.
Charles II was Archbishop of Lyons
between 1444 and 1488.

ANTOINE CARON
Beauvais circa 1520 — Paris circa 1598
Portrait of a Lady
Tempera on panel; 16 1/2″ × 13 1/2″.
Initialed and dated in upper right:
"AC. Ao. 1577."

this face and is underscored by the shafts of chiaroscuro that warm the pallid oval. Antoine Caron was one of the most important court artists during the turbulent reigns of Charles IX and Henry III. His paintings, especially the mythological and allegorical subjects, subtly express the fantastic vision, the complicated etiquette and the bizarre and artificial standards of behavior at the court. In this portrait, for instance, the artist does not limit himself to giving the subject a personality, but takes satisfaction in loading her with a cryptic, cantankerous, almost baleful, but exceedingly vital expression.

NICOLAS POUSSIN. *Apollo and Daphne* and *Midas and Bacchus.*
These two canvases of the same provenance probably formed a pair, as they are identical in format, are related in theme and belong to the same moment in Poussin's career. The theme is subtly set forth, but goes beyond its mythological content: note the figure of Oblivion in the story of Daphne, which gives the scene a languishing pathos. In theme, the stories concern the Golden Age, one of the most strongly rooted literary ideals of the 17th century, and in effect that century's mode of looking at antiquity. The paintings were done during the decade after the artist's arrival in Rome (1625),

NICOLAS POUSSIN
Les Andelys 1594 — Rome 1665
Apollo and Daphne
Oil on canvas; 38 1/2″ × approx. 53 1/4″.

a time when baroque classicism in the city was accompanied by a vein of neo-Venetian taste, which led to a revival of interest in 16th-century Venetian painting, especially Titian's work. In composition the two canvases reflect each other, mirror fashion and are constructed as dynamic rectangles, which gives the scenes a courtly solemnity, one of the characteristic features of Poussin's art.

CLAUDE LORRAIN. *Departure of Hagar and Ishmael.* *p. 156*
With Poussin, Claude Lorrain was one of the leading 17th-century painters in classicism and in landscape. He also lived in Rome and was attracted by myth and ideal imagery. We know from the *Liber Veritatis* (a list of his pictures, illustrated with sketches, which the artist kept up-to-date to protect himself against fakes) that this painting had a pendant representing *Hagar and Ishmael in the Wilderness* (now also in the Alte Pinakothek), and that both were painted for Count Waldstein. It is pleasing to imagine this pair hanging in a sumptuous reception room that would emphasize the escapist and dream-like atmosphere of the paintings, rife with the cryptic charm of their infinite distances. The biblical scene takes place as if on the natural stage of a Greek theater, balanced on the left by an architectural wing of

NICOLAS POUSSIN
Midas and Bacchus
Oil on canvas; 38 1/2″ × approx. 53 1/4″.

155

classical aspect, and seen against a natural setting of land, woods, sky and water enveloped in the predominantly golden tone of the sun.

CLAUDE LORRAIN. *A Seaport.*

Another subject in Claude Lorrain's repertory is the marine view. This typical example shows the master's extraordinary skill in rendering the ephemeral sense of the fleeting hour by subtle nuances of light. The place is imaginary and the triumphal arch, inspired by the Arch of Titus in the Roman Forum, gives the note of ancient solemnity that is typical of the artist's pictures. They always show some trophies and reminders of classical antiquity, ranging from fragments of column drums and copings (as in the foreground of the preceding painting) to entire ruins. But the vision always has its realistic side and is full of details studied from life and nature. Its only true subject, however, is the landscape in its broad sweep, accompanied by the in-

CLAUDE GELLÉ called
CLAUDE LORRAIN
Chamagne 1600 — Rome 1682
Departure of Hagar and Ishmael
Oil on canvas; 41 3/4″ × 55″.
Signed: "Claude Gelle Roma 1668."

CLAUDE LORRAIN
A Seaport
Oil on canvas; 28 3/4″ × 38 1/4″.
Signed: "Claudio I.V.F. Roma 1674."

tricate play of light from the low sun, which sends sparkling reflections across the water through the morning haze.

JEAN FRANÇOIS MILLET. *Italian Landscape.*   *p. 158*
The classicizing taste for landscape, launched by Poussin and Claude, was carried on by their imitators. It had a great vogue, which found expression in the following century in the view paintings of Gaspar van Wittal and Giovanni Paolo Panini. One of the less known of these landscape painters is J. F. Millet, Flemish by birth and Parisian by adoption, whose career was brief. In this landscape (probably of the Lombard lakes), the lesson learned from Claude Lorrain is evident in the awesome atmospheric sweep and the planes going back in measured recession until they are lost in the clouds. The popularity of this genre suggests the importance of the 17th-century discovery of Nature as an independent subject for painting, in which the representation of human beings becomes secondary, anecdotal and mar-

JEAN FRANÇOIS MILLET
Antwerp 1642 — Paris 1679
Italian Landscape
Oil on canvas; 41 3/4″ × 46 3/4″.

ginal. Here there is the greatest difference between Millet and Claude: this is no longer an ideal but a pure landscape; no longer historical painting, but a sensitive and evocative impression of nature.

JEAN–BAPTISTE SIMÉON CHARDIN. *Girl Peeling Vegetables.*
J. B. S. Chardin was the greatest interpreter of realism in France during the Enlightenment. A pupil of Cazés and an assistant of Coypel, Chardin was soon attracted to Flemish painting, turning from a decorative taste to an interest in the real, in the manner of Le Nain. Thus, he molded a simple yet elegant style of his own for the representation of daily and domestic life. Beyond the discovery of reality in a low-keyed and bourgeois sense, there was a coherent visual discovery, a new manner, absolutely shorn of pictorial ostentation, perfectly adapted to his view of life. Characteristic of his work is the sobriety of this painting, with its light and transparent impasto and its blended and attenuated tones. In construction, the image is always clear yet full of nuances, and the details of form have a caressing quality. Over all there is the artist's kind eye for subjects excluded from the academic genres, which are elevated to a great dignity by the strictness of the style.

FRANÇOIS BOUCHER. *Nude on a Sofa.*   *p. 160*
With respect to Chardin, François Boucher represents the right wing of 18th-century French painting. As is known, the artist — a pupil of Watteau — had a successful professional career which culminated in his becoming director of the Gobelins tapestry factory. He was also official court painter

JEAN–BAPTISTE SIMÉON CHARDIN
Paris 1699 — Paris 1779
Girl Peeling Vegetables
Oil on canvas; 18″ × 14 1/2″.

and director of the Academy. His life represents the final course of rococo taste, and his death coincides with the moment in which the style was yielding to the new severity of neoclassicism in all the capitals of Europe. This picture is a typical example of the kind of painting in vogue until after the middle of the century, for the decoration of intimate rooms. The girl, lying in a relaxed position that is between the sweet and the sensual, has an absorbed air; her figure attracts the eye like a precious object. The allusion of the disordered bed is a generic invitation, and is at the origin of an infinite number of subsequent odalisques. But it is a refined and intellectual invitation, because of the beauty of the feminine thoroughbred, on the one hand, and the grace with which the painting dissolves the material aspect of the image, on the other. It is the sophisticated product of a visual world created by Rubens and filtered through a century of pictorial experience.

FRANÇOIS BOUCHER
Paris 1703 — Paris 1770
Nude on a Sofa
Oil on canvas; 23 1/4″ × 28 3/4″.
Signed lower left:
"F. Boucher 1752."

HISTORY OF THE MUSEUM AND ITS BUILDING

HISTORY OF THE COLLECTIONS

The Alte Pinakothek, Munich's gallery of old masters, is so named to distinguish it from the Neue, or New, Pinakothek, the city's gallery of modern art, which contains works of the second half of the 19th century. (There is also the Neue Sammlung — New Collection — of contemporary art.) One of the most notable collections of paintings from the 15th to the first half of the 19th century, the Alte Pinakothek embodies the acquisitive efforts of the Bavarian House of Wittelsbach.

This great pictorial heritage is made up of a number of sizable accessions. A large group of baroque paintings, originally in the princely collections of Kurss-Kurpfalz and Pfalz-Zweibrücken, includes the largest number of works by Rubens in Germany and a series of masterpieces by Van Dyck and Rembrandt. The Italian pictures of the Early and High Renaissance are select, but more limited in number. Examples of the German masters collected by the reigning dukes were supplemented after Napoleon's restrictions on church property by the inclusion of such great works as Michael Pacher's *Four Fathers of the Church,* Dürer's *Four Apostles,* etc. In addition, the painters of all the principal countries are represented, for the Alte Pinakothek has a decidedly European character, in keeping with the history of Bavaria. In fact this duchy and kingdom, whose Elector Karl Albrecht became Holy Roman Emperor, was autonomous until 1871, when it joined the new Prussian-led German Empire. The gallery's international representation of course includes Flemish paintings, and among these Rogier van der Weyden's *St. Colomba Altarpiece* is outstanding. Although there is nothing by the van Eyck brothers in the collection, their example made panel painting important in Germany and they enjoyed the patronage of John of Bavaria, Bishop of Liege and Count of Luxemburg, Brabant and Holland.

But it is with Wilhelm IV (1493–1550), who unified the duchy, that the line of great Bavarian art patrons begins. He commissioned a number of German artists to decorate his pleasure house in the old rose garden of the Residenz at Munich. The decorative scheme, which includes pictures celebrating the deeds of famous men of antiquity, belongs to a conception of court art originating in the Middle Ages. Of these works, the gallery has the portraits of Duke Wilhelm and his duchess (1536) by Wertinger, Altdorfer's *Battle of Alexander,* Burgkmair's *Esther and Ahasuerus, The Story of Lucretia* by Jörg Breu the Elder and the *Discovery of the Cross* by Barthel Beham. Seven other panels, by Burgkmair, Jörg Breu the Elder, Jörg Breu the Younger, Feselen and Refinger, were installed at Schleissheim. Another group of these paintings — Schöpfer's *Mucius Scaevola* and Refinger's *Horatius Cocles* and *Manlius Torquatus* — was carried off to Sweden during the Thirty Years' War and is now in the National Museum at Stockholm. Cranach's *Lovers* and Hans Schöpfer the Elder's *Judgment of Paris,* in the same museum, come from the Duke of Bavaria's Kunstkammer.

The first collection as such, however, was formed by Albrecht V (1550–1579) who was a dedicated collector, especially of curiosities and rare objects of art and nature — following the custom of the time — and whose Schatzkammer ("Treasure") was the greatest in the world. His paintings were mainly portraits,

162

of princes and princesses, and of wise and famous men. Nevertheless, the important pictures besides those of Wilhelm IV, among the 700 items in the inventory of 1598, number at least a dozen, including Dürer's *Lucretia* and Altdorfer's *Susanna and the Elders*.

Maximilian I, who became Elector Palatine (1623) in the wake of the Battle of the White Mountain, was an admirer of Dürer. Without spending much, in fact without spending anything, he obtained such great works by the artist as the *Paumgartner Altarpiece,* from the church of St. Catherine in Nürnberg, the *Lamentation over the Dead Christ,* from the Predigerkirche and the *Four Apostles* from the Town Hall in the same city. At the same time, works by Rubens were beginning to enter the collection, for a letter written by the painter to Sir Dudley Carleton refers to the large *Lion Hunt* that he supplied to the Duke of Bavaria.

Ferdinand Maria (1651–1679), who married Adelaide of Savoy and thus was in touch with Italian artists, devoted himself to decorating his castles of Munich and Nymphenburg and the church of the Theatines, rather than to collecting single works of art. With the reign of his son, Maximilian II Emanuel (1679–1726), however, the collection of paintings became one of the first in Europe. On his visits to the courts of Spain, France and Germany he made so many acquisitions that more space to hang the pictures was needed, and he commissioned a new castle with ample galleries to be built at Schleissheim, by the Italian architect Zucalli. As Stadtholder of the Netherlands, he found himself in a position to buy Flemish and Dutch works in wholesale quantities. In 1698 he acquired a lot of 101 choice pieces in Antwerp for 90,000 guilders. These included twelve works by Rubens (*Portrait of Helena Fourment,* landscapes and other paintings now scattered among various collections) and fifteen by Van Dyck (some of these have been dispersed but the others include the *Portrait of the Organist Liberti, Portrait of the Painter Wael and His Wife, Portrait of the Architect Colyn de Nole, The Wife of Colyn de Nole and Her Daughter* and *The Duke and Duchess Von Croy*). The works bought in Antwerp also included Snyder's *Lioness Fighting a Wild Boar,* hunting scenes by Fyt and Boel, still lifes by De Heem and Jan Bruegel, as well as paintings by Wouwerman, Murillo, etc.

In the Schleissheim inventory for 1761 we find few Italian pictures, but these include such important works as Titian's *Charles V Seated* and *Profane Love,* and Paris Bordone's double portrait, among others. The number of Rubens' paintings is increased by the *Massacre of the Innocents, Meleanger and Atalanta, Peter and Paul* and the full-length *Portrait of Helena Fourment;* while the additional Van Dycks comprise the Malery, Ruthwen, Spinola and Mirabella portraits and the *Rest on the Flight to Egypt*. Besides the eleven Brouwers, there are seventeen Teniers, a couple of dozen Jan Bruegels and some fifty other Dutch paintings. In 1788 there are three Murillos, their acquisition probably connected with Maximilian II Emanuel's aspiration to obtain the crown of Spain for his son, who however predeceased him. Indeed this great collection, and the enormous expense entailed in amassing it, were intended to increase Maximilian's prestige, on a par with such political ambitions as his

163

aims in the War of the Spanish Succession. His grand political designs had their continuation in the policy of his son Karl Albrecht (1726–1745), who contended with Austria for primacy in Germany, with varying success, attaining the imperial crown but then seeing his dreams dissipated by the Treaty of Füssen (1745).

With the death of Maximilian III Joseph (1777), the Bavarian line of the Wittelsbachs was extinguished, and Karl Theodor of Sulzbach became King of Bavaria. Not a willing resident of Munich, he left his picture gallery in Düsseldorf but had a building constructed in Munich where the Bavarian collection could be displayed for study by art lovers and young artists. To the collection he added Dutch cabinet pictures like Jannssens' *Woman Reading,* and in latter years he moved the paintings of the Mannheim gallery to Munich. Assembled by Karl Philip, the last of the Pfalz-Neuburgs, this collection had been enlarged by Karl Theodor. It included some eight hundred pictures of the principal schools, with many Dutch works: two Rembrandts — *Holy Family* and *Sacrifice of Isaac;* paintings by Bol, Brouwer, the Ostades, Dou and Mieris; Ter Borch's *Boy Picking Fleas from a Dog,* Steen's *The Brawl* and Eliasz' so-called *Portrait of Admiral Tromp.* The German school was represented by several works of Elsheimer, and among the Flemish paintings were Rubens' *Shepherds,* the *Rape of the Sabine Women* and *Portrait of the Artist's Mother;* Van Dyck's *Portrait of Snayers* and *St. Sebastian;* and at least twenty cabinet pictures by Bruegel and Balen, including *Flora,* which had been executed in collaboration with Rubens. There were also Italian and Spanish works, among them a Carlo Dolci and Murillo's *Boys Eating Fruit.*

When Karl Theodor died in 1799, he was succeeded by Maximilian IV Joseph of the Pfalz-Zweibrücken branch (Maximilian I of Bavaria), who brought a third picture collection to Munich. The Zweibrücken collection had undergone many vicissitudes during the Revolution and its original 2,000 items had been reduced to half. Still it retained its character, which had a strong bent for French art. In fact the collection included landscapes by Claude Lorrain, Chardin's *Girl Peeling Vegetables,* Boucher's *Nude on a Sofa,* Greuze's *Young Girl* and pictures by Poussin, Le Brun, Le Moine, Le Prince, Subleyras, Desportes, etc. No Rubens figures among the Flemish paintings, but there were eight Teniers. The Dutch pictures were numerous and fine: the Ruisdaels, Ostade, Wouwerman, Berchem, the De Heems, Metsu's *The Cook,* etc. With the secularization of church property in Bavaria and the Tyrol, which was then Bavarian, there was another influx of works of art. Especially important among these new acquisitions were paintings of the old German school from Kempten, Ottobeuren, Benediktbeuren, Tegernsee, Kaisheim, Ulm and Wettenhausen. At the same time there were some more recent works of outstanding quality, such as Tintoretto's great *Crucifixion* from the church of the Augustinians in Munich, Rubens' *Woman of the Apocalypse* from the Cathedral of Freising and Tiepolo's *Adoration of the Magi* from the Convent of Schwarzach in Franconia. Meanwhile, the contents of the Düsseldorf Gallery, which Maximilian I decided to move to Munich in 1805, had progressively grown through a variety of acquisitions. Pictures had come in from the castles of Dachau, Neuburg and Haag which were evacuated between 1803 and 1804. Then there was the incorporation of the galleries of the free cities of Bamberg, Augsburg and Nürnberg; while other works came from the marquisate of Ansbach and a number were donated by Aschaffenburg. Düsseldorf had come to the Palatinate through the marriage of Duke Ludwig Philip of Neuburg-Sulzbach to Anna, daughter and heiress of Duke Wilhelm of Jülich and Berg. Their son, Wolfgang Wilhelm, who married a daughter of Wilhelm V of Bavaria, was in touch with Rubens and Van Dyck. From the former he acquired the *Large Last Judgment* in 1618; and in 1620, three pictures formerly destined for the church of the Jesuits in Neuburg. He was in personal contact with Van Dyck, and from him acquired his *Portrait with a Dog*. The correspondence with Rubens still exists; it does not appear from these commissions that Wolfgang Wilhelm was thinking of creating his own gallery. His descendant, Johann Wilhelm (1690–1716), who resided exclusively in Düsseldorf, achieved this naturally through the Dutch and Italian painters he had at court — van Douven, van der Werff, Weenix, Ruijsch, Zanetti, Bellucci and Pellegrini — who were employed in decorating the castle of Bensberg. Acquisitions were made with an open hand, and then a substantial addition to the collection resulted from the marriage of the Duke to Maria Luisa de' Medici. Although there were no more than 350 works in the collection, these were all masterpieces. Of the more than forty Rubens in the Alte Pinakothek, more than half come from Düsseldorf, as do more than half the thirty Van Dycks, the two secular subjects by Jordaens, three of the finest Snyders, six of Rembrandt's biblical series and his *Self-Portrait*, as well as Flemish and Dutch cabinet pictures. Among the Italians, besides the Carracci, Domenichino and Reni, Tintoretto's so-called *Vesalius,* Andrea del Sarto's *Holy Family* and Raphael's *Canigiani Holy Family* all come from the Düsseldorf collection.

Throughout the period discussed, works of art underwent innumerable misfortunes and adventures, whether in the Bavarian collection or in others whose formation was similarly tied to the political problems of an ambitious state. In any case, every art work has its own story, the ins and outs of which are pleasurable to retrace. Here we must limit ourselves to sketching the broad lines in the development of the Munich heritage. At this point there remains only to add that with the political void in 19th-century Bavarian history, the new kingdom's art vocation turned again to collecting in its narrow sense, which at the most is an indication of taste. In effect the gallery's activity was limited to exchanges and purchases. Its documents of the early 19th century again show the names of famous dealers (Leprieur, Lucchesi, Artaria) and news of acquisitions and exchanges (Potter for Ribera, Dürer for Mengs, etc.).

Around 1808 the gallery began to buy Italian 15th- and 16th-century works of art. The accounts of all the successive and disparate acquisitions have been preserved, but certainly the most interesting are those ordered by Ludwig I, which were based on an organic historical and cultural concept. Among other works acquired at this time were paintings by Fra Filippo Lippi and Filippino Lippi, Botticelli, Ghirlandaio and Perugino, Raphael's *Tempi Madonna* and the *Madonna della Tenda*. It was the first half of the 19th century, and these names will suffice to show how up-to-date the selections were. The rest is recent history.

LEGEND

1 GERMANY

2 PICTURES OF THE 16TH CENTURY

3 PICTURES OF THE 17TH CENTURY

4 ALTDORFER

5 DÜRER

6 GRÜNEWALD

7 FLANDERS

8 HOLLAND

9 FLANDERS

10 RUBENS AND VAN DYCK

11 FLANDERS

12 ITALY

13 ITALY

14 SPAIN

15 TITIAN

16 FRANCE

THE BUILDING

The Alte Pinakothek's present building is a large and imposing edifice in the neoclassic style. Designed by the architect Leo von Klenze, who was also responsible for the Propylaea and the Glyptothek in Munich, it was built between 1826 and 1836. Ludwig I, who ordered the reorganization of the Pinakothek, promoted the project. Von Klenze's constructions and others commissioned by the King give the Munich townscape of the period a completeness in keeping with Ludwig's philhellenic tastes.

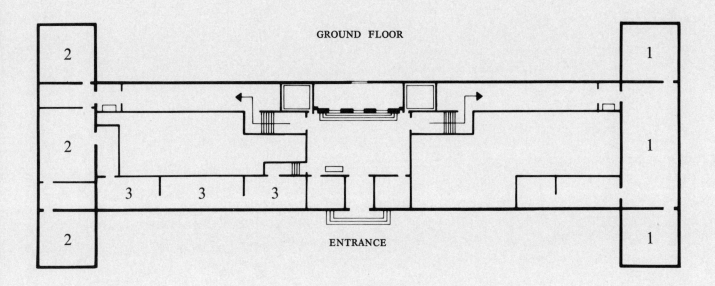

GROUND FLOOR

ENTRANCE

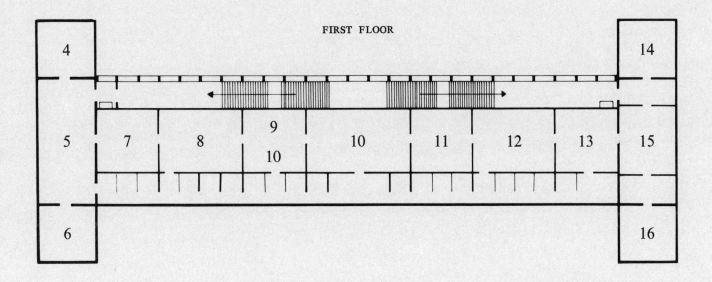

FIRST FLOOR

SELECTED BIBLIOGRAPHY

BENESCH, OTTO. *German Painting: From Dürer to Holbein.* (Skira, Geneva; World Publishing Co., 1966).

BERGSTRÖM, INGVARD. *Dutch Still Life Painting.* tr. by Christine Hedström and Gerald Taylor. (P. Joseloff, New York, 1956).

BODE, WILHELM VON. *Great Masters of Dutch and Flemish Painting.* tr. by M. C. Clarke. (Duckworth, London, 1909).

BRION, MARCEL. *German Painting.* (Universe Books, New York, 1959).

BUCHNER, ERNST. *Art Treasures of the Pinakothek.* (Abrams, New York, 1957).

BURCKHARDT, JAKOB C. *Recollections of Rubens.* tr. by Mary D. Hottinger. (Phaidon, London, 1950).

CUTLER, CHARLES D. *Northern Painting.* (Holt, Rinehart & Winston, New York, 1968).

DELEVOY, ROBERT L. *Early Flemish Painting.* (McGraw-Hill & Co., New York, 1963).

DESCARGUES, PIERRE. *Cranach.* (Harry N. Abrams, New York, 1961).

FLETCHER, JENNIFER. *Peter Paul Rubens.* (Phaidon, London, 1968).

FRIEDLAENDER, MAX J. *From Van Eyck to Brueghel.* (Phaidon, London, 1956).

FROMENTIN, EUGENE. *The Masks of Past Time: Dutch and Flemish Painting from Van Eyck to Rembrandt.* tr. by A. Boyle. (Phaidon, London, 1948).

GROSSMANN, F., ed. *Brueghel, the Paintings: Complete Edition.* (Phaidon, London, 1956).

LASSAIGNE, JACQUES and DELEVOY, ROBERT L. *Flemish Painting.* (Skira, New York, 1958).

LEVEY, MICHAEL. *Dürer.* (W. W. Norton & Co., New York, 1961).

MAUROIS, ANDRE. *An Illustrated History of Germany.* tr. by Stephen Hardman. (Viking Press, New York, 1965).

MEYER, EMIL R. *Dutch Painting: Seventeenth Century.* (McGraw-Hill & Co., New York, 1962).

PANOFSKY, ERWIN. *Albrecht Dürer.* 3rd ed., 2 vols. (Princeton University Press, Princeton, 1948).

PANOFSKY, ERWIN. *Early Netherlandish Painting.* (Harvard University Press, Cambridge, 1954).

PEVSNER, NIKOLAUS and MEIER, MICHAEL. *Grünewald.* (Abrams, New York, 1958).

ROSENBERG, JAKOB. *Rembrandt.* 2 vols. (Harvard University Press, Cambridge, 1948).

RUHMER, EBERHARD. *Cranach.* (Phaidon, London, 1963).

SHIPP, HORACE. *The Flemish Masters.* (Philosophical Library, Inc., New York, 1954).

STANGE, ALFRED. *German Painting, XIV–XVI Centuries.* (Macmillan, New York, 1950).

WAETZOLDT, WILHELM. *Dürer and His Times.* (Phaidon, London, 1950).

For her courtesy in furnishing information for the preparation of this book, the editors wish to thank Dr. Liselotte Camp, Director of the Museums of Munich.

INDEX OF ILLUSTRATIONS

Page

169

INDEX OF NAMES

GENERAL INDEX